THE
CULTURAL
APPRAISAL OF
DEVELOPMENT
PROJECTS

THE
CULTURAL
APPRAISAL OF
DEVELOPMENT
PROJECTS

GLYNN COCHRANE

PRAEGER PUBLISHERS
Praeger Special Studies

New York • London • Sydney • Toronto

Library of Congress Cataloging in Publication Data

Cochrane, Glynn.
   The cultural appraisal of development projects.

   Includes bibliographical references and index.
    1. Economic assistance--Evaluation. 2. Technical
assistance--Evaluation. 3. Intercultural communication.
4. Economic development projects--Evaluation.
I. Title.
HC60.C54   338.9'007'23   78-31130
ISBN 0-03-047586-4

PRAEGER PUBLISHERS
PRAEGER SPECIAL STUDIES
383 Madison Avenue, New York, N.Y. 10017, U.S.A.

Published in the United States of America in 1979
by Praeger Publishers,
A Division of Holt, Rinehart and Winston, CBS, Inc.

9   038   987654321

Printed in the United States of America

For Brendan, Siobhan, and Rory Kevin

ACKNOWLEDGMENTS

Personal service with the Ministry of Overseas Development (ODM) in the United Kingdom and consultant experience with the World Bank (IBRD) and the U.S. Agency for International Development (AID) in Washington, D.C. provided opportunities for me to try to apply my social science training to project work. I am indebted to many people in those organizations: in the ODM, to Derek Cudmore, "Bim" Davies, Jim Tedder, and Tom Russell; in the IBRD, to Bernard Chadenet, John King, Mudie Birney, and Warren Baum; and in AID, to Dan Creedon, Jonathan Silverstone, Robert Berg, Edward Cohn, and Dick Blue.

Ruth Willis typed the first draft of this book; Gail Fuller typed the second; and Barbara Miller helped by proofreading. I would also like to thank Mary Ann Keenan of the State University of New York at Oneonta, Michael Horowitz of the State University of New York at Binghampton, David Brokensha of the University of California at Santa Barbara, Francis Lethem and Michael Cernea of the World Bank, Polly Harrison of Catholic University in Washington, D.C., and my colleagues at Syracuse University, Jim Vedder, Dennis Rondinelli, Pauline Atherton, Michael Barkun, and Guthrie Birkhead—all of whom made comments on early drafts.

While what I have written does not necessarily reflect the views or opinions of those who have helped, it inevitably reflects their support and encouragement.

CONTENTS

LIST OF TABLES

LIST OF FIGURES

LIST OF MAPS

1 INTRODUCTION

CHANGES IN DEVELOPMENT ASSISTANCE POLICY

In the years since World War II, religious groups and voluntary organizations like OXFAM and CARE have been concerned with providing prompt assistance to those who need it most. These efforts concentrate on medicines, food, clothing, and shelter for the poor.[1] Multilateral and bilateral aid usually have had the longer-term objective of developing the economy, thus decreasing the future need for development assistance. These officially sponsored efforts concentrate on projects of an infrastructural nature: irrigation, cash crops, livestock, roads, dams, and bridges.

AID's Response

For a quarter of a century following the end of World War II, the U.S. Agency for International Development (AID) and the World Bank (International Bank for Reconstruction and Development, IBRD) gave loans to Third World countries to construct, plant, and market the kinds of things they believed would cause economic growth.

Immediate giving to alleviate suffering, on the one hand, and longer-term development plans and objectives, on the other, appeared to complement each other. However, by the late 1960s the development assistance community in the industrial nations had become increasingly worried because official assistance was not achieving its development objectives, for the rich in the Third World became wealthier as the poor became more impoverished. The policy of transferring technology and finance from the rich nations to the developing countries had not worked as well as had been anticipated.

With the idea of achieving a more equitable distribution of the benefits of development assistance, a new series of objectives and priorities for development assistance have been proposed. Efforts are now to be concentrated on the most disadvantaged people in the Third World, those previously bypassed by aid. These are the people referred to as "marginal"–the "bottom 40 percent." Of course, in some countries the miserably impoverished are the bottom 80 or even 90 percent. The new policies aim to introduce better education, effective population programs, better nutrition programs, as well as economic programs to raise incomes for the most distressed. Aid is now supposed to get where it is most needed.[2]

Reflecting the shift in U.S. thinking, the administrator of AID, in an internal memorandum during January 1972, stated that

> programming economic assistance more directly to meet basic human needs, rather than primarily for overall country growth, will be and essential feature of our redirected AID. . . . We have learned that if development is truly to occur, it has meaning only to the extent that genuine benefits accrue to those in lower levels of the social and economic order.

U.S. bilateral foreign assistance programs since World War II, like the multilateral programs of the UN agencies, had been characterized by an emphasis on economic growth, measured in terms of increase in per capita GNP. This increase was seen as being necessary to overcome the effects of increases in population, to provide a surplus for further investment, and, if possible, to establish a growth in consumer goods and services. Social development was usually linked with economic development and consequently expressed as "economic and social development."[3]

During the growth-model era, economists believed that benefits might not be equitably distributed during the initial stages of economic growth, but that eventually they would be shared by all; that is, the "trickle down" or "spillover" effect would occur. In the meantime, economic development would be served by devoting relatively small amounts to the creation of social and physical infrastructure through fostering community development, increasing the size and improving somewhat the quality of schools, spreading preventive health services, and so on. Benefits did not trickle down, however. Instead, increasing economic growth caused increasing social inequality.[4]

World Bank's Responses

Robert McNamara, president of the World Bank, commissioned a report on recommendations for future directions in aid giving from Lester Pearson and a number of prominent development thinkers.

McNamara knew that population, education, and nutrition were linked with economic growth; furthermore, he had planners who convinced him that an attack on poverty caused by overpopulation, illiteracy, and malnutrition would make sense in banking terms. Among the first things that Robert McNamara did on assuming the presidency of the World Bank was to support lending for population and education programs (he also appointed an environmental adviser in 1971). Barbara Ward cites McNamara's remarks at the annual meeting of the Bank's governors in 1971:

> Among the 2 billion people living in the more than 100 developing countries the Bank serves, there are hundreds of millions of individuals barely surviving on the margin of life, living under conditions so degraded by disease, illiteracy, malnutrition, and squalor as to deny them the basic human necessities. These are the "marginal men," men and women living in "absolute poverty." It is clear that development efforts of the past, both by governments and by the Bank, have simply not made an adequate contribution to the welfare of this huge and growing group.[5]

The same sense of priorities has been growing in developing countries. As a communique produced at a Third World Forum, meeting in Karachi, January 5 through 10, 1975, said:

> The real focus should be on the satisfaction of basic human needs and on a meaningful participation of the masses in the shaping of economic and social change; the policies of self-reliance should be encouraged, with emphasis on a self-confident and creative use of local resources, manpower, technology and knowledge, and with a growing stress on collective self-reliance between the societies of the Third World; the concepts of development should embrace the political needs and cultural patterns of their societies, so that life styles in the Third World do not become a pale imitation of somebody else's experience but a proud extension of their own value systems.[6]

THE LOGISTICS OF CULTURAL APPRAISAL OF PROJECTS

This book is directed toward those with responsibility for the identification, design, and implementation of Third World development projects; projects whose benefits are intended to reach the poorest in those countries. The focus is primarily on the role of the project manager in both the public and private sectors and, to a lesser extent, on relationships among participants, social scientists, and nonproject officials; and on the ways in which those relationships help or hinder the project process.

To achieve the goal of better development projects one must steer between the Scylla of "real world" concerns and the Charybdis of scholasticism. The author has been giving guidance on the cultural appraisal of development projects for almost 20 years, first as an administrator with British development assistance, then as a consultant for U.S. AID and the World Bank.[7] His experience has inclined him to the view that standards of cultural appraisal will improve if the focus of efforts to improve is upon the project process and how project managers and social scientists can work together. A message directed either to social scientists or project managers alone would be inadequate.

Social scientists and project managers have different work habits. A project manager concerned with projects must constantly give opinions and form judgments in an imperfect world. What the civil servant often wants is a social scientist who is prepared and able to give informed judgments and opinions in a manner that can be understood during the early stages of project design, and who is prepared to concentrate not only on past problems with a particular project but also on suggestions for better projects in the future.

Social Science and the Project Process

What social scientists need is a methodology to help them know the kinds of issues and information that should be communicated to project managers. Social scientists are often reluctant to commit themselves until they have all the necessary data. The academic wants to see greater use made of social science methods and techniques that show a high probability of contributing to alleviation of pressing human problems. However, it is not realistic to expect that every development project can receive expert social science scrutiny. Therefore, social scientists must learn to communicate more effectively with project managers.

Project Managers and Social Science

Also needed is a methodology that permits project managers to know, more than they do at present, when they need help from social scientists. There are standard tests for projects on financial, economic, and environmental grounds.[8] The same standardization can be useful for cultural analysis. Too few social scientists are involved in a systematic manner in project work. For example, a population project in one country, or part of a country, may have a manager who feels he needs a social psychologist; the same type of project in another country or area can have a project manager who does not feel the need for any social science input. Cultural appraisal is too often ad hoc or ad hominem.

Cultural Appraisal Capacity in Developing Countries

It may seem odd that officials in Third World nations often need help in undertaking cultural appraisal in rural areas of their own countries. They need to be able to organize, analyze, and focus the skills they do have. It is frequently the case that these officials have been trained overseas and that in their own countries they have lived in social environments far removed from those that are to be affected by projects. Many of those who work for bilateral or multilateral development assistance agencies are also more familiar with social conditions in industrialized countries than they are with the lives of those who have been by-passed by previous development assistance efforts in rural areas of the Third World.

Cultural factors can no longer be thought of as extrinsic to project design; project design has to conform to and take account of the social landscape. Cultural factors are project design. This means that the role of the project manager assumes a new importance. Either project managers will conduct cultural appraisal of projects themselves or, recognizing that a project has certain complexities, they will obtain social science expertise. Therefore, the project manager's skill in making an initial determination about the cultural aspects of a project is critical.

A METHODOLOGY FOR CULTURAL APPRAISAL

The decision to allocate resources within a developing country to particular projects that will benefit particular types of people is inevitably influenced by political considerations. This book concentrates on what should happen after such decisions have been made. Before individual projects can be identified, the nature, location, and magnitude of social distress must be analyzed in a cultural context. National plans and country programs, which are considered in separate chapters, often rely too much on macroeconomic data and have in the past said little about social and cultural characteristics of the people. This information must be obtained if cultural appraisal is to be satisfactorily executed. Social mapping techniques that can be used to disaggregate and overcome these deficiencies are explained in Chapter 3.

In Chapter 4, the author suggests that a standard series of criteria for handling cultural factors be created for project design. These criteria could be used by social scientists in structuring advice so that it can be appreciated by project managers. They might also be used by project managers in determining need for expert social science help.

Chapter 5 describes principles and processes of implementation, seeking to emphasize the changes in project implementation that occur as a consequence of increased consideration of cultural factors. This chapter also provides standardized criteria that can be used to improve the relationship between social scientists and project managers. Discussion stresses the advantages of adopting an experimental approach toward projects designed to reach the poorest.

Many project managers want to know how to obtain good quality data and timely consultant guidance: many Third World countries already have the necessary resources, but these are not used to full advantage at present.

Advice on how to select and brief social scientists for project assignments and how to interpret their reports is provided in Chapters 6 and 7. Comments are also made on the advisability of obtaining different kinds of social science expertise.

No magical formulas emerge. There can be no assurance that the guidance given here, if followed, will result in better projects and more situations where poor people can participate in the benefits of development projects. There are many instances where people have changed, and will continue to change, despite minimal attention having been paid to their culture. Such neglect is not only morally and ethically reprehensible, it is also poor planning. Experience has shown, however, that it is more useful to pay attention to culture, and resources are wasted if this is not done.

The author should make it clear that he does not regard Third World people in rural areas as necessarily irrational or fatalistic. In many instances responsibility for lack of change in the circumstances of very poor people rests with governments at national or local levels. Sometimes donors who say they want to help the poorest people in developing countries continue to finance projects whose main beneficiaries are the already well-off. Practically, however, one knows that development projects represent an opportunity for change that must involve both community members and central or local government officials. This book aims to show some of the possibilities for cultural adaptation and innovation among community members and the ways in which project procedures must change in order to achieve a mutually beneficial working relationship.

In the absence of any operationally useful theory of social change the best that can be done is to produce a project system made up from a series of criteria that, if assessed by project managers, increase chances for project success. The cockpit drill a pilot performs before takeoff is not a theory about flight, or takeoff; rather, it is a safety device to minimize risks. The method here advocated for the cultural appraisal of projects is similar. What is needed is a system that can, at the same time, increase project managers' awareness of cultural factors and increase social scientists' awareness of the requirements of the project process.

This book is not intended to present an account of how detailed, in-depth, and finished social science or project management analyses actually look. The intention is not to turn project managers into social scientists or vice versa; the intention is to create conditions where social scientists and project managers can collaborate in order to implement their shared concern for project quality.

The appraisal system presented in this book can accommodate varying levels of project complexity; that is, it can be used by project personnel engaged in international missions on behalf of bilateral or multilateral development assistance organizations, by Third World civil servants, or by officials of voluntary organizations acting as project managers in remote rural areas. The system has also been designed to accommodate different levels of manpower skills, that is, an international team or a local team. Experience has also shown that cultural appraisal can be integrated with other project analyses—financial, organizational, and economic—without any undue delay or increase in cost.

NOTES

1. Peter Williams and Adrian Morris, *Not by Governments Alone: The Role of British Non-Governmental Organizations in the Development Decade* (London: Overseas Development Institute, 1964).

2. *The Role of Popular Participation in Development* (Cambridge, Mass.: Massachusetts Institute of Technology, 1968), Report no. 12. Discusses Title IX of the United States Foreign Assistance Act, 1966.

3. For an account of economic bias in past UN activities, see their *Social Development in Asia—Retrospect and Prospect* (New York: United Nations, 1971), paras. 1-13.

4. Influential books concerned with this problem were: Robert E. Asher, *Development Assistance in the Seventies, Alternatives for the U.S.* (Washington, D.C.: Brookings Institution, 1970); Rutherford M. Poats, *Technology for Developing Nations: New Directions for U.S. Technical Assistance* (Washington, D.C.: Brookings Institution, 1972); Andrew Schonfield, *The Attack on World Poverty* (New York: Vantage Books, 1962).

5. See Barbara Ward, *The Rich Nations and the Poor Nations* (New York: Norton, 1962). Influential papers included, for example, Frank Notestein, "The Population Crisis: Reasons for Hope," *Foreign Affairs* 46, no. 1 (October 1967); a Conservation Foundation paper on the environmental dangers of international development, Thayer Scudder, "The Unforeseen Ecologic Boomerang" (Garden City, N.Y.: National History Press, 1968).

6. Reuters News Service, January 11, 1975.

7. The author served as an administrative official with the British Ministry of Overseas Development in the South Pacific from 1961 until 1967. During the last ten years he has worked on development projects in Thailand, the Philippines, Liberia, Nigeria, Papua New Guinea, Colombia, Peru, Haiti, Tanzania, and Morocco. A sabbatical year in Washington with AID produced *Social Science Training and Manpower Development* (Washington, D.C.: AID, 1974), which contributed to the agency's institution of the Development Studies Program (DSP) and a decision to hire anthropologists. He wrote the section on "social soundness analysis,"used by AID, in its *Project Manual* (Washington, D.C.: AID, 1974), to analyze the cultural aspects of projects. A year-long association with the central projects division of the World Bank with a former student, Raymond Noronha, resulted in a report, *The Use of Anthropology in Project Operations of the World Bank Group* (Washington, D.C.: Central Projects Division, International Bank for Reconstruction and Development, 1973).

8. See, for example, Warren C. Baum, "The Project Cycle," *Finance and Development* 7, no. 2 (June 1970); James Price-Gittinger, *The Economic Analysis of Agricultural Projects* (Baltimore: Johns Hopkins University Press, 1972).

2 CULTURAL FACTORS IN PROJECTS

Comprehensive project information dealing with cultural factors is not normally available. Even when available it may not be used. Many project managers feel that there is little order and structure in cultural accounts, and their project managers' attempts to simplify such accounts have not been notably successful. The nature of cultural information can be bewildering for project managers and, consequently, important factors, from the point of view of projects, may be overlooked in what appears to be a universe of data. The project manager searches in vain for a norm, the average—some form of standardization.

The social scientist searches for the unique response that university life rewards, yet this means that five social scientists asked to give an opinion about the same project might well give five different responses. This does not give project managers much assistance or confidence. Therefore, project managers tend to use social scientists for confirmation, to "gild the lily." A small number of social scientists capable of dealing with cultural factors now do project work, but they are often used in self-defeating ways; for example, the social scientists are consulted after the main features of project design have been decided.

Socially relevant projects are small and messy and may well go wrong. There is pressure in many development assistance organizations for large "show-all" projects requiring large sums of money.[1] Social scientists and their concerns are thought to delay projects too long and to complicate projects unnecessarily.

EMPHASIS ON THE MANAGEABLE ASPECTS OF PROJECTS

Attention is often focused during the life of projects only on physical infrastructure—the building of dams, construction of clinics—and on the amounts of money obligated:

The emphasis on investment expenditure as a propellant of development, though misleading, is comforting. It absolves people, especially those responsible for policy, from considering the possibilities and costs of operating on the basic determinants of material advance. It encourages the facile belief that such advance is possible without the qualities, attitudes, and efforts which it has required elsewhere—in other words, that economic development is possible without cultural change.[2]

Obviously, there is a need to pay systematic attention to cultural factors in projects. Development projects are intended to create opportunities for poor people to make a better way of life for themselves. Those who are burdened by large families are offered contraceptive facilities; those who have low incomes are offered employment or the chance to produce more crops. What is important is not the fact that there may be need for a project, as appreciated by national or international civil servants, but that, through appropriate project design and implementation, people can and will take advantage of the project opportunities offered to permanently change their lives. Unless popular attitudes toward contraception are altered and remain altered after the project is over, a population project will fail. Unless official methods of appraising the cultural dimensions of projects change, such projects will continue to fail.

Another example of inadequate cultural appraisal concerns the need for low-income housing in St. Louis, Missouri, in the 1960s, which was met by constuction of the Pruett Igoe complex. Vandalism and crime reached unbearable levels. It was the failure of the designers to anticipate that tenants would not adjust their behavior to unfamiliar high-rise living that eventually forced the abandonment of the project.[3] Sociological research before construction might have revealed the inappropriateness of such housing for the community involved.

IMPLICIT THEORIES ABOUT CHANGE

Although seldom stated in such a way, it is a fact that all development projects are founded on the premise that one can predict and produce social change. The theory of social change contained in most development projects is quite simple—a combination of need and supply: if people who want money are shown how to get it, they will adjust their behavior accordingly; if people who have suffered from disease and malnutrition are shown better ways, they will adopt those ways. Each project contains an explicit or implicit statement about how social change may be accomplished.

Increasing prices for agricultural produce, demonstration of benefits, or erection of facilities are commonly thought of as ways to produce social change. Since World War II and the rise of economic analysis in project work, the prevailing theory among project managers for social change, insofar as it has been explicitly stated, has been based on economic "rationalism" and the presumed logic of the situation.[4] People with no money are presumed to want jobs, those with large families are thought to desire contraception, ambitious parents are assumed to want education for their children, and so on. However, it is doubtful if such assumptions can be universally made:

> What the native of any country, and the representative of any culture is ultimately, even if unconsciously, interested in is self-assertion and self-expression. He may want some of the advantages of civilized knowledge, but he will inevitably want to make use of them in the rhythm of his life and in a society he has inherited even if it is a modified society![5]

If the lives of very poor people in Third World societies were similar to those of poor people in industrialized countries it would be useful to assume that decisions would be made by project participants to maximize their monetary returns if given an opportunity to do so. However, where conditions are not comparable because cultural factors differ from those of industrial countries, the persistence of a "rational" theory of change leads to misunderstanding that can affect projects adversely. People in developing countries do not always want the kind of life that people in industrialized countries want, as illustrated by the following story:

> Wahinua went to work for the agricultural officer at Kira Kira as a cookboy in 1960, a short while after the death of the "big man" in Tawani village. At the same time Wahinua's two nephews joined the Public Works Department in Kira Kira as labourers.
>
> They worked for six years until they had saved enough money to buy thirty pigs; then they stopped work and returned to Tawani village. All moneymaking activities in Tawani village ceased. No copra was made because all the coconuts were required to make puddings, and no vegetables could be taken to Kira Kira market because they were also needed for the feast.
>
> Wahinua had always been an extremely hard-working man and, over the years, through entering into a large number of reciprocal relationships, and as a result of shrewd marriages he had a large number of people obligated to him. By calling on these people at one time to repay their obligation Wahinua was able to organize the giving of a feast.
>
> A very large feast was made and Wahinua gained the status of "big man." The total cost of the feast, which lasted only for one day, was $1,200. Wahinua had had a choice: instead of making his feast, the

amount of money he had saved through hard work over the years could have been used to purchase European goods. But Wahinua had chosen the status of "big man" rather than the kinds of goods that had made up the "cargo" of "Marching Rule." This experience raised a doubt as to whether the Solomon Islanders really had a Europeanized pattern of material wants. In Wahinua's case possession of status had been more important than possession of wealth.[6]

COMMON ERRORS DUE TO CULTURAL VARIATION

In this chapter a case is made for raising the existing level of cultural appraisal of development projects. Failure to assess adequately the importance of cultural variation can be broken down into three common kinds of error (with some obvious overlapping): ignoring factors of sufficient magnitude to make it unlikely that a project will achieve its intended effect, making false assumptions about culture that preclude project success or minimize long-term results, and utilizing false measurements or statements that exaggerate project impact.

Ignored Factors

When cultural variation is ignored and analysis leading to corrective action does not occur, projects may fail to reach their goals; for example, if people do not use irrigation waters, this may be due to cultural factors and not simply to poor engineering of the ditches.[7] Assumptions that are basic to project success may be insufficiently tested; for example, when it is assumed that sufficiently high price incentives to increase agricultural production will end local resistance to change. Insights that might increase project replication may be missed if project staff believe that, when contraceptive technology is more fully developed, population growth can be controlled effectively. Causes for failure to achieve project verification are often cultural rather than technical. Opportunities are lost when cultural factors are ignored.

Two decades ago, culture was seen as an obstacle, a barrier to be overcome. Those subscribing to this approach talked about "change agents," that is, project personnel who could be sent into areas to change culture: "Studies . . . called one set of persons 'planners,' 'initiators,' or 'change agents.' . . . The other set . . . were simply supposed to accede, gratefully to the well-intended ministration of the former."[8]

In the same vein, there is still some talk about "human constraints on development," that is, the existence of supposedly inappropriate attitudes, beliefs, and values, as well as complementary institutional structures. The results of that kind of thinking are projects like Hilton hotels. Each hotel, no matter in what country it is located, has more or less the same construction, more or less the same facilities. The concession that is made to location is usually to have porters and doormen in colorful local garb and to have a few local rugs and artifacts in the lobby area. In the same way, projects dealing with roads, agricultural credit, and so on, when designed by persons who ignore cultural factors, turn out to be similar in most countries. People who believe in fitting universal project designs into particular cultures ask in what way a country conforms to their previous experience. The more important question is: In what way does a country depart from previous experience?[9] Technical soundness is vital to projects; but when technical considerations dominate to the exclusion of cultural factors, there is a danger that cultural factors affecting participation will be ignored.

Cultural Values Clash with Project Values

There are social conventions that discourage participation in development projects. In parts of South America some peasants regard increases in material possessions as antisocial. In such communities, the popular view is that the good things in life are in short supply. Each person should receive a share of the good things of life. Anyone who acts in such a way as to do better than his or her neighbors is thought to be acting in an antisocial manner. This concept is referred to as the "image of limited good."[10]

Fatalism and Apathy

Uruguayan livestock projects aimed to provide stock and fencing subsidies to very poor people in an effort to raise income and improve nutrition. However, the people concerned possessed a strong sense of fatalism that made their participation impossible. Fatalism has, in other parts of South America, made very poor people turn away from resettlement projects, since joining such projects requires a certain amount of confidence. In India, the existence of a similar belief —that poverty and illness are one's inevitable, God-given fate—has made poor people avoid medical facilities or participation in economic development projects. Of course, not all poor people possess either fatalism or the sense of "limited good," but enough do to warrant investigation of such cultural factors.

The manager who says that he wants to help the poorest but does not alter his project design to make allowances for the debilitating consequences of poverty is engaging in a classic instance of "moving the target to hit the bullet." Inability to innovate or adapt is not always the outcome of a belief system; it may be produced as a consequence of hunger and malnutrition, or poor project design and implementation. Those who have not eaten and are weak cannot make the same kinds of buoyant, confident, entrepreneurial decisions as the well-to-do. Persons who have been bypassed by previous development assistance projects may have little confidence in official assistance and are not likely to risk their meager resources on an official project.

Hostility and Strife

Cultural factors can intrude even where poor people do wish to participate in development projects. The Wainoni land development projects on the island of San Cristobal in the South Pacific gave landless peasants 20 acres of land and provided coconut seedlings and agricultural advice in order to increase cash income. The project was also to absorb immigrants from crowded inland acres. From the start the project was plagued by litigation that was so tedious and protracted that several years passed without project goals being reached. Eventually, the project had to be abandoned. The litigation over land boundaries was handled by local courts, which appeared unable to resolve the problems.

Conflict was all the more odd to the government since the 20-acre plots had been meticulously laid out by government surveyors using the latest methods. What went wrong? Settlers came from bush areas high in inland mountain ranges. Each man had an ancestral shrine in the middle of his land that he would visit on a regular basis. Peasants defined the boundaries on their ground by its center. They practiced shifting cultivation in a circle around the shrine. The outer perimeter of the ground was not defined. The need to visit the shrine and family food needs defined plot size. Thus, the people failed to grasp the new conception of squared-off boundaries, and endless understandable conflict arose. This practice of defining plots by their center rather than by imaginary boxlike lines on the property also has been noted in Africa and South America.[11]

Participation Calls for Abnormal Response

A population project in South America failed when it relied on condoms as the sole contraceptive technology: among those people, men used condoms only with prostitutes, so the project was doomed through choice of inappropriate technology. A project to build maternity clinics on South Sea islands started by local midwives failed through unsuspected causes. People in the area were promiscuous. Tradition required a woman to reveal the names of her lovers just before giving birth. Failure to confess was thought to expose the woman to malpresentation of the fetus, or she might be seized by a shark while bathing in the sea. Women were unwilling to confess to a local midwife. The problem was solved when midwives from other islands were brought in to staff the clinics.[12]

Rationalism is not universal. For example, following World War II Britain needed all the eggs the country could get for a war-torn, hungry population. The most efficient way to get those eggs was known to involve the battery system, that is, placing hens in small cages, force-feeding them, and regulating the lighting. The British did not take to the system because they felt it was unduly cruel to animals. A similar exercise of irrationality caused a malaria eradication project to founder in West Africa. People would not return from their gardens or workplaces to open their houses for spraying teams. People were avoiding the sprayers despite the fact that they did not like malaria. They had discovered that DDT spray, when left on the walls, eventually entered the bodies of small lizards. Lizards were then eaten by pet kittens. The DDT attacked the central nervous system of the kittens and they died. People liked their pets more than they wanted the benefits of the malaria eradication program, but they were anxious not to offend powerful government officials and so did not tell them.

Incentives for Participation Are Meaningless

Ignorance of social arrangements often leads the designers of projects to assume that the society they are dealing with is an institutional wilderness either possessing no institutional structures suitable for economic and social development or possessing institutions considered less suitable than those that serve industrial countries. In a Sierra Leone agricultural project to create marketing facilities, an elaborate government-run organization was created. The new structure ignored the entrepreneurial role played by women's voluntary associations in West Africa, and resources were wasted. A road maintenance project in Afghanistan foundered because maintenance crews were made up on a countrywide basis. Men on maintenance crews often had to travel long distances from home and had to spend considerable periods of time away from home. Afghanistan has a number of highly independent ethnic groups and members of each group like to stay near their homes. The problem was alleviated when road crews were localized and made responsible for road maintenance within their own ethnic areas.

A European businessman was trying to conclude a deal in an Indian bazaar for delivery of 1,000 brass trays. The price in the bazaar being 12 rupees apiece, he asked what the delivered price would be for his bulk order. He was amazed to hear the trader say it would be 15 rupees a tray, and asked why this was so. The trader replied that that was to compensate him for all the extra inconvenience.

Many housing projects have wasted scarce resources because of insufficient attention paid to local living arrangements. For example, housing projects in India put the kitchens outdoors, with the result that the kitchens were not used because cooking facilities should not be in a separate building.

Nutrition projects have failed in South America on many occasions because planners did not appreciate the difference between "cold" foods and "hot" foods. Some foods that are thought to be "cold," such as fish, cannot be eaten in the evening. The idea of "hot" and "cold" varies but has great influence on people's dietary patterns.[13] Many South Americans also think that vitamins are very powerful, and it is difficult to get pregnant women to take vitamin supplements. Projects paying insufficient attention to cultural factors have produced the wrong kind of flour for making tortillas and have tried to induce people to drink milk, which they felt was bad for their health.

False Assumptions

Unfounded assumptions make it impossible for projects to reach their goals. In Peru during the 1968 reform movement, land was taken from the very rich landowners and managed by the army. Benefits of the land reform were eventually supposed to be felt by the impoverished, landless day laborers. However, under the management of army officers productivity fell sharply in about 30 percent of the expropriated areas, thereby worsening the conditions of landless day laborers. With respect to those latifundia, government had failed to appreciate that rich people are not simply rich because they have money. Rich people are, in part, successful because they are rich in skills, education, and so on. Poor people, on the contrary, are often poor in skills. Reform movements can take money from rich people and give it to poor people, but they cannot instantaneously take skills from rich people and give these skills to the poor. Any project concentrating on social change by means of the transfer of physical resources from rich to poor is probably unwise.

Some nutrition projects have failed because the manner of food distribution within households was not understood and was assumed to be equitable. For example, in Jamaica men get the largest share of meat at the family meal. There is no point in concentrating on increased food production unless the increase will reach those who need the food most.[14] The unfounded assumption behind many projects intended to improve nutrition is that the benefits are reaching the right people.

Employment Produces Negative Effects

Unfounded assumptions about culture are perceived as good things, so much so that they are often not vigorously checked. For example, employment is assumed to be beneficial in any kind of project and any location. Employment is usually questioned only on its economic merits: Would capital-intensive methods be preferable to labor-intensive methods?

Yet, there are, inevitably, negative effects stemming from increased employment, since the social dimensions of employment are almost always ignored. Where employment forces migration, as in southern, eastern, middle, and western Africa, an extra burden is placed on women. The crime rate in villages denuded of able-bodied males may increase. Employment tends to be directed toward males at the expense of female participation. Employment, as Lord Hailey first noted in his *African Survey*, also serves to weaken ties between generations in traditional areas undergoing rapid social change.[15] Young men are no longer dependent on their elders for bride price; old men have few ways to gain money and so lose power and prestige. Tension between generations increases, and old people are no longer cared for by their relatives. As Raymond Apthorpe states, "This stratum . . . most depends on traditional social relations of kin and mutual aid . . . ; [nonworking older] peasants suffer most when these are abrogated, just as they are least able to withstand the depredations of tax collectors or landlords. [16]

What relevant skills and attitudes are created and sustained through employment generated by projects? Little of permanent value may accrue to communities wherein projects are located. An example is employment created by road projects sited in an agricultural community. The skills and techniques learned on the project are not of a kind that participants will find useful in their normal agricultural pursuits. Job requirements of a project should integrate with job requirements for males in the project community once a project is terminated, otherwise the belief that employment effects are a benefit may be unfounded.

Road projects in western Kenya assumed that wages earned in construction and maintenance would be used to buy food and to provide the necessities of life for the workers' families. In fact, wages were usually gambled away and large sums were spent on beer.[17] Patterns of expenditure of wages are, like other cultural patterns, the product of experience. It is too often assumed by project designers that project participants will immediately adopt the expenditure patterns of laborers in industrialized countries. However, for people who have not lived by using money, the first attempts to do so can be harrowing. Many recent immigrants to cities quickly become malnourished. In rural areas they did not have to buy their food. Faced with the problem of buying food, they often spend too much on foods with little nutritional value.[18]

Model Participant Is Not Representative

In many cases project design assumes that participants can reach the level of productivity of outstanding individual farmers. Projects to grow bananas in Fiji and coffee in Kenya both used successful independent farmers as their model participants. It was assumed that, given the project opportunities, others could reach the same level of productivity. But the successful individual entrepreneurs in many of those instances were persons who had severed their social ties. They did not feed or lend money to their poor relatives—they did not share what they had. Those models of behavior were responsible for a level of economic performance that project designers considered worthy of emulation, while local people saw a pattern of social performance that was considered deviant.[19] Accumulation of resources is only one side of the coin—distribution systems that meet local convention are equally important in project design.

Benefits Are Not Used as Anticipated

Agricultural projects in Papua New Guinea concentrated all their publicity on how producers who sold more could afford to buy material goods. While production increased, profits were used to buy trucks to take relatives to market, boats to take friends fishing, or they were spent on large parties. Resources were not invested but were distributed conspicuously in accordance with traditional norms. The unfounded assumption was that, once increased productivity was achieved, consumer attitudes would change.

False Measurements

False measurements mistakenly assess the magnitude of social change produced by projects and the time taken to achieve those changes. Project design has inevitably reflected the cultural assumptions of industrial countries. One such prominent assumption is the need to have large projects with massive impact. While it is possible to see the intellectual attraction of such conceptions as "takeoff into economic growth," "redistribution with growth," "the green revolution," or "reaching the poorest overseas," a convincing case can be made that these are cultural manifestations of industrial countries. These theories are popular, in part, because they show the intellectual potency of industrialized countries. Development ideas promising immediate and dramatic breakthroughs have always been popular in industrial countries, back to the days of the infamous groundnut schemes of the British in East Africa.

It is difficult for industrial countries to comprehend the hopelessness of a situation in which progress in handling the problems of Third World countries may have to be measured by how little the situation has degenerated, rather than by how much one has advanced. The cultural antecedents of industrial countries lead to the assumption that the application of science and technology, allied with the fruits of experience, can improve any situation.

Projects often promise much more than they can realistically achieve—inflated claims are made, effects are exaggerated. This is understandable, since project papers are not to be considered scientific documents, but rather documents of advocacy, aiming to persuade.

Time Required for Social Change

Most projects are supposed to last from three to five years. The life span of a project is obtained by estimating how long it will take to complete the physical dimensions: buildings and bridges take time to construct, fertilizer may have to be applied and a certain level of productivity may have to be achieved, people may have to be trained. The duration of a project is usually determined by such calculations.

In Africa, Asia, and South America projects repeatedly fail when advisers and funds are withdrawn before participants have learned to manage on their own. For example, a resettlement project in the Pacific took Gilbertese from the

Central Pacific and left them in the fertile Solomons. Each family was given a plot and expected to grow its own food as well as some cash crops. Agricultural advice was kept to a minimum because the ground was so fertile and local people could assist the settlers. After some months, the project was a clear failure and the settlers had to be put on rations. The translation from coral atolls to volcanic atolls, from scratching out a bare living to abundance, was more than could be quickly mastered.

Project managers often have to design projects without any clear idea of suitable project duration. A project to introduce wet rice-growing techniques into Liberia would, it was thought, undoubtedly produce benefits, since existing dry rice production techniques were inadequate for the country's needs. But Liberians do not like wet rice techniques. How long would adoption take? Projects were mounted before any answer to this question was known. The project failed within the budgeted time period.[20]

Importance of Cultural Impact

All projects are supposed to have a substantial impact on critical problems or needs. The justification for a project tends to be the contribution that it can make to the broader situation. If this contribution is to be made, then two things must happen: very poor people need to be involved as participants and the kinds of innovation or adaptation represented by the project must have a potential to spread to other areas with similar problems.

In the Caqueta resettlement project in Colombia, each settler was to be given title to ten hectares of land if he followed the directions of the extension service. Settlers were selected from among those who had already shown that they could help themselves. Those selected were then given official assistance under the provisions of the project. From a management point of view the decision to help those who had demonstrated that they were "worthy" of help seemed sound. From a development point of view this selection of participants was less acceptable.

If assistance went to those who had demonstrated self-sufficiency, what would happen to those who were not selected? If the well-off were to be given project assistance, how were the very poor to catch up? If the well-off were outstanding and were helped, what was to happen to those who were not outstanding? The logic used by managers selecting participants made for a successful project, but it also necessarily lessened overall impact of the project.[21] If development is indeed the contribution made to the overall situation, it would seem that a project could be a success in economic and social terms used in conventional project analysis and yet be a failure in terms of its contribution to development.

NOTES

1. Judith Tendler, *Inside Foreign Aid* (Baltimore: Johns Hopkins University Press, 1975).

2. Peter T. Bauer and Barbara Ward, *Two Views of Aid* (Bombay: Vikas, 1966), p. 49.

3. John Turner, *Freedom to Build* (New York: Macmillan, 1972), p. 267.

4. John King, *Economic Development Projects and Their Appraisal* (Baltimore: Johns Hopkins University Press, 1967), for the World Bank; Albert Hirschman, *Development Projects Observed* (Washington D.C.: Brookings Institution, 1967).

5. Richard Thurnwald, "The Price of the White Man's Peace," *Pacific Affairs* 9, no. 3 (1937).

6. Glynn Cochrane, *Big Men and Cargo Cults* (Oxford: Clarendon Press, 1970), pp. 9-12.

7. Jasper Ingersoll, *The Social Feasibility of Pa Mong Irrigation* (Washington, D.C.: AID, 1959).

8. Raymond Apthorpe, "Planners and Planistrators in Eastern Africa, 1960-1970," in *Development from Below*, ed. David Pitt (The Hague: Mouton, 1976).

9. Cyril Belshaw, "Social Structure and Cultural Values as Related to Economic Growth," *International Social Science Journal* 16, no. 2 (1964).

10. George Foster, "Peasant Society and the Image of Limited Good," *American Anthropologist* 67 (1965).

11. Glynn Cochrane, "Choice of Residence in the Solomons and a Focal Land Model," *Journal of the Polynesian Society* 78, no. 3 (September 1969).

12. Glynn Cochrane, "Conflict between Law and Sexual Mores on San Cristobal," *Oceania* 40 (September 1969).

13. Personal communication from William Mangin.

14. Ann P. Den Hartog and Arnold Bornstein Johansson, "Social Science, Food and Nutrition," in *Development from Below*, ed. David Pitt (The Hague: Mouton, 1976).

15. See also Apthorpe, "Planners and Planistrators."

16. Ibid.

17. Personal observation.

18. Den Hartog and Johansson, "Social Science."

19. Cyril Belshaw, *Under the Ivi Tree* (Berkeley: University of California Press, 1964).

20. Personal communication with UNDP officials in Liberia.

21. Ralph Roberts, *Migration and Colonization in Colombian Amazonia* (Syracuse, N.Y.: Syracuse University Ph.D. microfilm); and communication with IBRD officials.

3 SOCIAL MAPPING

We have seen in Chapter 2 that before projects can be identified and designed appropriately the nature of the cultural landscape must be known. The first step in creating a means of systematizing treatment of the cultural dimensions of projects is the undertaking of a national inventory of cultural resources and human needs. Attitudes, values, and beliefs should be viewed as important resources for adaptation and change, rather than as constraints and obstacles. Such an inventory serves a number of functions.

A knowledge of cultural resources can highlight those problems that can and should be solved, given the level of resources available. Decisions about project location may become easier, as may those concerned with project size. In essence, such an inventory can create, at the national level, the cultural equivalent of macroeconomic data.

Most national development plans fail to take important cultural factors sufficiently into account. As a consequence, there can be waste when a social scientist is initially asked to analyze the cultural dimensions of a project. The social scientist must relate local project considerations to national considerations. This information is usually more available to economists than to noneconomists. Projects may not be located in the best areas—those areas with the greatest number of poor. Projects may lack replication or spread effects. Many of these consequences can be attributed to a failure to collect and analyze macrolevel cultural data before turning to project identification.

CRITERIA FOR STANDARDIZATION AND CONVERGENCE

Some degree of uniformity and predictability is necessary in evaluation of the cultural dimensions of projects. This can increase project managers' ability to recognize both situations requiring social science expertise and those where appraisal can be carried out with existing resources. The range of social sciences is considerable and there is wide variation between types of social scientists. Standardization and convergence between project managers and social scientists can be achieved by interrelating criteria to form a common reference framework. Criteria should lend themselves to quantitative, as well as qualitative, interpretation. These criteria would constitute a national inventory of cultural resources, and must be established before project decisions are taken.

Project managers can then ask that social science consultants fit their reports to the criteria. Social scientists, in using such criteria, will have a clearer idea of the kinds of information sought at the macro- and microlevels, even though individual social scientists may have limited familiarity with the development organization. Project managers can then, also using the criteria, be more confident about contracting for, evaluating, and using the consultant reports.

The criteria for a national inventory of cultural resources are as follows:

Identification of groups—seeking the identification and location of social groups.
Social organization—describing types of indigenous social organization.
Belief systems—evaluating the significance of ideological considerations for the project process.
Wealth forms—describing types of wealth people try to accumulate, and their functions.
Patterns of mobility—seeking the establishment of patterns of movement for potential project participants.
Access to basic human needs—creating an analytical description of the poorest together with an assessment of the causes of extreme poverty.

The inventory process produces macrolevel social data, focused on the poorest people in the country. It is vital to appreciate that, at minimum, each of the criteria must be satisfied. Unless this is done, the ensuing project design may well be faulty. These criteria are interrelated in ways that have vital consequences for project design. Instead of cultural dimensions being thought of, as they too often are, after the main details of project design have been decided, cultural factors must become an important part of project design. They are intrinsic, not extrinsic, variables.

IDENTIFICATION OF GROUPS

If scarce project resources are to be allocated efficiently to achieve maximum impact at minimum cost, then the number, identity, and location of potential project participants must be analyzed. Most potential project participants living in rural areas of Third World nations derive cultural identity from member-

MAP 3.1

A Tribal Map of Tanganyika

Tribal boundaries from *Atlas of Tanganyika,* 3rd Ed., 1956, with revisions according to Dr. P.H. Gulliver, "A Tribal Map of Tanganyika," *Tanganyika Notes and Records,* No. 52, (March 1959) pp. 61−74, and other sources.

MASAI

0   100   200
Miles

Source: *Atlas of Tanganyika,* 3d ed. (Tanganyika: Tanganyika Notes and Records, 1956), with revisions according to P. H. Gulliver, "A Tribal Map of Tanganyika," *Tanganyika Notes and Records* 52 (March 1959): 61-74. Used with permission of the author and *Tanganyika Notes and Records.*

ship in ethnic, religious, or political associations. Social groups in a country should be identified and mapped out if they appear to be distinctive groups (as are the Hindus versus the Muslims), with mutually unintelligible languages, opposing political parties or tribal groups, or different ethnic identities—groups that, for some reason, act on the basis of a perception of their difference from other groups. See Map 3.1 for an example of tribal groupings. When tensions exist, each group may need a separate project. For example, in Liberia it would not be possible to mount a project that included Mande speakers, Mandingos, and Christians. Tensions among the groups are considerable and cooperation could only be achieved at great cost. Where tensions are great, special project design will be necessary.

Group Delineation Defines Project Parameters

Sometimes well-known divisions are not sufficiently articulated in projects. During project identification in North Africa, Berber, Tuareg, or Maghreb populations need to be distinguished from the descendants of Islamic expansion of the sixth and seventh centuries; in Nigeria there has been tension at times between the Islamic north and the Christian south of the country; in Sierra Leone there has been tension between the Mende and Temne people; in Fiji there has been tension between Indian descendants of immigrant plantation laborers and native Fijians. Other divisions are less well known. Medical extension work in India suffered when attempts were made to have extension personnel move between Brahmin and untouchable clients within the same village.

Population figures must be disaggregated and replaced with numbers tied to distinctive groups. Since social cleavages are in many instances stronger than the ties, it is never sufficient to give aggregate data, such as that "x" thousand live in the northeast region. Delineation of social groups should also indicate the size of the populations involved: these may range from hundreds of thousands, such as the Ashanti or Zulu of Africa, down to a few hundred, as in the case of an Australian aboriginal band or group of bushmen in the Kalahari Desert.

Group Delineation Indicates Project Impact

Occasionally, the differences are vital for project outcome. For example, a project to resettle the entire three villages of the Phoenix Islands was threatened with failure when the Protestant villages refused to cooperate with the Catholic village. The question arises: Will a project designed with the social characteristics of one group in mind have a beneficial impact on other groups that are not on friendly terms with the project participants?

Group delineation is necessary to identify potential spread and replication effects of projects. Unless group delineation takes place, claims about the possible impact and spread effects may be highly inaccurate. For example, if it is claimed that 60,000 people will benefit from a project because that is the regional population, yet social mapping shows that there are only 20,000 in one group and no friendly contacts with groups in contiguous areas, social mapping will be useful in checking the accuracy of project claims. Social mapping is very important during identification and design of projects.

Countries such as Tanzania and Kenya have excellent rural surveys capable of providing this type of information. In other instances, social mapping may take from two months to a year to accomplish. Social mapping should be entrusted to experienced social scientists (see Chapter 6).

SOCIAL ORGANIZATION

Rather than assume that existing institutions and forms of organization are inappropriate, it is necessary to assess the nature and scope of those structures so that every opportunity may be taken to use what already exists. Using familiar organizations is much less wasteful than creating entirely new structures. Relationships involving property and the production and distribution of goods and services are important. Are land and property, movable and immovable, held by tribes, lineages, families, or individuals?

Property Holding

Where projects create or attempt to change property rights, these changes should relate to the existing environment.[1] Inheritance patterns are uniform in industrial countries, but this is not the case in most Third World countries. Generally speaking, rights to immovable property descend either through males (patrilineal) or through females (matrilineal). Both matrilineal and patrilineal patterns of inheritance, in their traditional forms, may be found in a country alongside the pattern common to industrial countries. Matrilineal and patrilineal property systems involve related members of a tribe, clan, or lineage. See Map 3.2 and Table 3.1 for examples of nonindustrial-type inheritance patterns.

Muslim patterns of inheritance in many countries emphasize division among all eligible heirs. On occasion this can result in excessive fragmentation of property. Even single trees have been subject to this law: one writer noticed an entry in the Sri Lanka deeds registry for one three hundred and forty-sixth of a yak tree.[2] This inheritance pattern is the product of a time and place in which different circumstances prevailed.

Forms of property holding need to be mapped out for the country, focusing on areal distribution. Once this has been determined, an assessment of experience with "partibility"—the breakup of group or family property through indi-

MAP 3.2

Land Use Related to Land Tenure, Smallholders in Bukoba, Tanzania

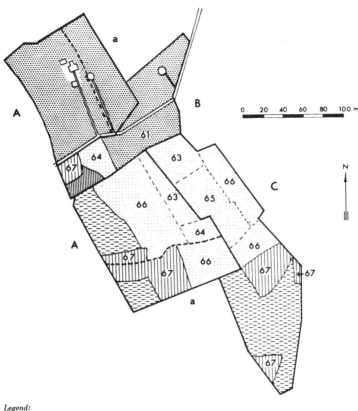

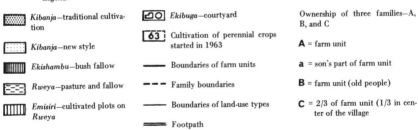

Legend:

Kibanja—traditional cultivation

Kibanja—new style

Ekishambu—bush fallow

Rweya—pasture and fallow

Emisiri—cultivated plots on Rweya

Ekibuga—courtyard

Cultivation of perennial crops started in 1963

— Boundaries of farm units

- - - Family boundaries

— Boundaries of land-use types

Footpath

Ownership of three families—A, B, and C

A = farm unit

a = son's part of farm unit

B = farm unit (old people)

C = 2/3 of farm unit (1/3 in center of the village

Source: Jorgen Rald and Karen Rald, *Rural Organization in Bukoba District, Tanzania* (Uppsala, Sweden: Scandinavian Institute for African Studies, 1975).

TABLE 3.1

Land Use Related to Land Tenure, Smallholders in Bukoba, Tanzania

Land Use	Clan Tenure	Individual Tenure	Government
Kibanja (mainly perennial crops—banana and coffee)	*Acquisition* (a) By inheritance. (b) Allocation by consent of clan members. *Rights of Use* (c) Proprietary rights within the unwritten rules of the clan. (d) Usufructuary rights for family members according to head of family decision. *Transfer Rights* Within lifetime of holder, sale requires consent of clan; at holder's death transfer to heirs according to customary clan laws. Dividing among heirs. *Heirs* Male and female. (Formerly only males could inherit immovable property.)	*Acquisition* (a) By purchase. (b) Allocation by government (deserted *kibanja* with no claim from clan). *Rights of Use* (c) Proprietary rights within individual ownership rights: freehold. *Transfer Rights* Within the owner's lifetime free disposal. At owner's death land goes back to clan tenure and follows customary laws, inheritance and dividing among heirs. ⟵ *Heirs* As under clan tenure: male and female.	*Acquisition* Deserted *kibanja* with no clan claim: government takes over. Formerly taken over by the chief. *Transfer Rights* Allocation to individuals. Application required. ⟵

26

Ekishambu	Like kibanja.	Like kibanja.	Like kibanja.
Rweya	*Acquisition* Like kibanja a and b. (This kind of rweya is mainly adjacent to the kibanja and considered potential kibanja land.) *Rights of Use* (c) Free grazing rights for all cattle owners. (d) Omusiri cultivation: permission of holder; usually contribution to holder from crop. (e) Cutting grass: permission of holder. *Transfer Rights* Same as under kibanja. *Heirs* Male and female.	*Acquisition* (a) Purchase. (b) Allocation by government on government rweya *Rights of Use* (c) Free grazing rights for all cattle owners. (d) Omusiri cultivation: permission of owner contribution to owner. (e) Cutting grass: permission of owner. *Transfer Rights* Within the owner's lifetime free disposal. At owner's death land goes back to clan tenure. *Heirs* As under clan tenure.	*Acquisition* Unused land formerly held by the chiefs now held by government. *Rights of Use* (c) Free grazing rights for all. (d) Free omusiri cultivation to all. (e) Free cutting of grass for all. *Transfer Rights* Allocation to individuals Allocation to Ujamaa villages. Application required.
Omusiri	No special tenure for omusiri plots, as they are temporary and part of the rweya land-use pattern. For rights of use, see under rweya.		

Source: Jorgen Rald and Karen Rald, *Rural Organization in Bukoba District, Tanzania* (Uppsala, Sweden: Scandinavian Institute for African Studies, 1975).

vidualizing property concepts—needs to be undertaken. Partibility may cause distress, may create a class of landless peasants, and may be resisted. Is partibility really necessary? Property holding arrangements for projects in one part of the country frequently should differ from those of another area.

Grasping the nature of forms of social organization usually needs professional assistance. The biblical story of the prodigal son shows how property relations can be understood. The son demanded his share of family lands, wasted the proceeds, and returned home. His relatives were angry with him, but his father killed the "fatted calf." The anger of the other family members probably did not come from the wasting of resources or the prodigal son's return to ask for more, but for his heinous offense in asking that family lands be parceled.

Organization for Rural Development

Project managers must decide what form of organization to encourage. Is the family the farming unit? Are traditional lineage or tribal structures strong? What forms of work association are common? Organization of and cooperation in production and distribution of goods and services may be based on kinship, religious affiliation, or membership in political parties. The nature, type, and location of these forms of organization must be understood. The organization of Australian aboriginal bands reflects adaptation to their largely desert environment; the sparse settlements of Eskimo people reflect the same principle. The joint family in India reflects the work needs of family farming. Small nomadic bands in tropical rain forests are well suited to hunting and gathering, while the band structure of bushmen of the Kalahari Desert is similarly well adjusted to their environment.

Every project innovation has consequences for traditional work organization.[3] The key decision is involved with creating opportunities that use traditional forms of organization to the maximum extent. Projects that ignore local organizational arrangements are often unsuccessful. Individualized small-scale production may break up family groups. Family groups may be able to produce palm oil. Planatation agriculture may require a change in traditional residence patterns because lands are allocated to progressive individual entrepreneurs rather than to families. New irrigation systems or improved range management practices require a high degree of coordination and cooperation from beneficiaries.[4]

If the main characteristics of inheritance and social patterns are understood, projects can avoid creating conflicts with established or changing local norms. Scarlett Epstein, an anthropologist, described such a situation:

> With a bank loan guaranteed by the government a number of fermentaries were established in the Gazelle Peninsula of Papua New

Guinea. The Tolai Cocoa Project (TCP) was a non-profit making institution. Each Tolai grower who wished to have his wet cocoa beans processed and sold by TCP, registered with one of the fermentaries, which paid cash on delivery, kept a record of quantities involved and paid a final settlement after the consignment had been sold and operating costs deducted. In spite of its obvious advantages to Tolai cocoa growers and the pride they took in it, the project began to face serious competition from European and Chinese traders soon after its inception. The drift away took on increasing proportions. As Tolai cocoa production increased so increased the proportion sold to independent traders. According to the customary inheritance pattern a man's sister's son rather than his own son had first claim to inherit his property, crops, money and all. In order to circumvent the traditional pattern of inheritance and give their own sons a better start in life, many Tolai tried to avoid having records of their property and earnings: they planted part of their matrilineage land with cocoa without registering the trees and sold the wet beans clandestinely to Chinese traders who, unlike TCP, kept no record of payments. This enabled their sons to accumulate the proceeds from cocoa sales without leaving any evidence of the amounts involved. On the old man's death his own matrilineal kin would thus not be able to claim the money as theirs.

There were many conscientious and shrewd Tolai elders who were keen to insure the project's success and disliked the idea of selling their cocoa to independent traders for less money than the project paid. Yet they were caught in a dilemma and could not see a way out. The conflicting pulls, emanating from their customary inheritance pattern on one hand and from their attachment to their own sons on the other, account for the apparently irrational and irresponsible behavior of many dignified and respectable Tolai men.

On the basis of this analysis, Epstein postulated in 1969 that unless the project abolished growers' sales records, the drift away from the project would continue. Shortly after, the project was reorganized and sales records abolished. This successfully reduced the proportion of Tolai cocoa sold to independent traders.[5] Ron Crocombe has provided an organizational analysis of such societies, as follows:

Pacific island societies have neither the degree of internal cohesion provided by common religious and defensive goals, which facilitate extremely comprehensive cooperative action, as in Israeli *kibbutzim*, nor the powerful external sanctions of the Russian Kolkoz. There is, nevertheless, a strong disposition toward joint action, usually by kin-based groups, for particular purposes. There may be a case for cooperative land holding, the independent family farms held from the cooperative, giving security of groups' cohesion combined with freedom of individual action in the operation of the farm. . . . The evidence suggests, however, that exploitation of farms by a joint or cooperative work force is likely to be [unsuccessful].[6]

On the other hand, oil palm development has been a highly successful enterprise in Malaysia. In that country farmers are literate, their social structure permits cultivation of palms by residential family units, and there are sufficient land and capital to ensure that the projects can be widely replicated.

BELIEF SYSTEMS

The form and content of ideological systems determine the nature of the types of opportunities that can be offered by development projects. Muslim, Hindu, and Christian belief systems, for example, correlate somewhat with attitudes toward projects. What must be evaluated and mapped out at the national level is the effect of various belief systems on the relationship between sexes, modernization, reproductive behavior, health, and food patterns. Each ideological system presents different opportunities for change and adaptation. Ethnic and religious groups, living in different parts of the country, may have different attitudes and beliefs with respect to reproduction, health, or economic development.

Relationship between Sexes

Development projects have frequently placed women in a less favorable position than was traditionally the case. Women in rural areas have, in effect, been bypassed by the development process. Women have not been able to earn money in a convenient manner. Industrialization has usually given work to men instead of women because women cannot always leave their children. Furthermore, industrialization has often been restricted to the educated, and women have not had the same educational opportunities as men.

Women have been underrepresented in agricultural extension services. Though women may perform a great deal of agricultural work, projects have tended to ignore their role and have concentrated on males. Such negative effects on the status of women are among the unintended consequences of social change. For example, introduction of Christianity has often meant removal of a traditional taboo on sexual intercourse for two to three years following the birth of a child. One of the consequences of this is that female nutritional status has sometimes suffered.[7]

Attitudes toward Modernization

In addition to fatalism or the "image of limited good" mentioned in the previous chapter, there may be a range of different attitudes toward modernization. These may vary significantly depending on their geographical location with respect to political or religious associations. What are the desired symbols of modernization? Are they education and a white-collar job, material goods, money, access to better health, or opportunities to leave home and go to the city?[8]

If possible, peoples' desires should be ranked and recorded for the whole country, together with any significant variations. In this respect, it is important to see if women's wants are significantly different from those of men and if age differences elicit different patterns.

Attitudes toward Reproductive Behavior

In India there is evidence that anxiety to have a surviving son in areas with high infant and child mortality rates has been responsible for large family size. In other parts of Asia and South America a large family has been looked on as a form of insurance against old age. Family size may also be perceived as an indicator of male virility or female utility. Even a desire for immortality can affect reproductive behavior: in parts of East Africa a man who dies without issue is considered more dead than he who leaves heirs.

What is the social meaning attached to having or not having children in various parts of a country? Does family size vary significantly with the income of parents? Do rich or well-educated people have smaller families? Are religion and location significant factors?[9]

Attitudes toward Health and Food

Knowledge of belief systems may be an important prelude to satisfactory health projects. If disease is attributed to intrusion of an evil spirit in the body of the patient, the indicated solution is extraction of the offending spirit. If illness is thought to result from soul loss, manifestly the problem is one of restoring the wandering soul. In neither case is recourse to modern health measures a logical move. An awareness of the reasons behind such rejection of health services assists the professional personnel materially in taking advantage of opportunities to change and in substituting the concepts and practices of modern medicine for those of the traditional culture. It is generally easier to gain acceptance for modern practices, such as the use of injections, than it is to instill understanding of the concepts behind them; yet, until the latter is accomplished the graft of introduced medical culture is not genuinely established.

What types of food are popular and which are disdained? Local beliefs with respect to foods provide useful clues for those who prepare educational materials. Why is fish disdained? Perhaps because of religious attitudes it is not regarded as "true" food. The same may hold for pork and lard, as a consequence of which they are only slightly exploited, even though they are available. Prejudice also plays an important part in limiting diet and should, if prominent in a country, be recorded. Why does a mother refuse to give her small child cooked animal blood, even when the latter is plentiful, inexpensive, and obviously nutritious? It may be because she believes that the child who consumes blood will not learn to talk. Or perhaps the blood is considered more fit for sacrifice to the supernatural. Why is there a widespread prejudice against raising pigeons for food? Possibly it is because of the conviction that they bring bad luck to the household. Why, in some areas, are beans seldom eaten? It may be because they are thought responsible for liver ailments.[10]

WEALTH FORMS

Project managers have to consider what kinds of incentive are to be offered. The number of items that are considered to be wealth must also be mapped out on a national basis. Money income is measured in units that can be added, multiplied, divided, and so on, whereas criteria of well-being among very poor people are often collective in nature and cannot be thus quantified.[11] This suggests the inadequacy of global quantitative assessments of income without complementary qualitative interpretation of social and geographical groupings that reflect distinct social meanings, as assigned by those whose circumstances are quantified.

Inadequacy of Monetary Measurement Alone

Many things that affect the well-being of very poor people are not in the market: cultural integrity and social or community solidarity, parent-child relationships, religious attitudes. The performance of traditional rituals can be thought of as income. Similarly, health, nutrition, and education benefits are not materialistic or quantifiable. Individual money incomes may be high or low and this fact is not easily or obviously related to the availability of and satisfaction with health, education, or nutrition services. These group sentiments are characteristic of many traditional societies and, once eroded, cannot easily be replaced.

Income distribution figures do not usually show how income is distributed with respect to variables such as ethnicity, social class, education, aptitude, geographical location, and so on. Each society has a set of religious, political, and ethical rules—some formal, some informal—that determine who gets what, and

TABLE 3.2

Priorities of Household Expenditure Items

Table 39. 60 expenditure items in 16 main groups

Food
1. Meat
2. Fish
3. Banana (eating)
4. Banana (*pombe*)
5. Vegetables
6. Onions
7. Spices
8. Salt
9. Sugar
10. Fruit
11. Bread and cakes
12. Cassava
13. Sweet potatoes
14. Rice
15. Maize
16. Maize flour
17. Other flour
18. Beans
19. Groundnuts
20. Cooking oil
21. Eggs
22. Millet, sorghum

Food (*cont.*)
23. Meals outside the house
24. Other food
Drink
25. Local beer
26. Bottle beer
27. Milk
28. Tea (coffee)
29. Banana juice
Cigarettes and the like
30. Cigarettes, snuff
31. Sweets
32. Chewing coffee
Personal articles
33. Personal articles
34. Soap
35. Paper, books, and the like
Household equipment
36. Household equipment
37. Furniture
38. Firewood
39. Coffee trading
40. Matches and the like

Clothes (41.)
Bicycle (42.)
Transport (43.)
Medicine, hospital fee (44.)
School fee (45.)
Society fee (46.)
Social contributions (47.)
Religious offerings (48.)
Court cases (49.)
Investments in house and farmland
50. Housebuilding
51. Tools
52. Manure
53. Grass
54. Cattle dipping
55. Hired labor
56. Other expenses
Money transactions
57. Repaying debt
58. Moneylending
59. Coffee trading
60. Other

The ranking of the expenditure items according to the number of households spending money on the various items, regardless of the amount used, gives a first impression of priorities. Table 40 shows the items where all 25 households had expenditure.

Table 40. Priorities of expenditure items I

Items	Number of Households	Range in Shares per Year	Average Shares per Year
1. Meat	25	3-99	48
8. Salt	25	2-24	9
34. Soap	25	2-56	19
39. Kerosene	25	2-36	13
41. Clothes	25	5-249	100

(continued)

33

TABLE 3.2 *(continued)*

Table 41 continues the ranking of expenditure items according to the numbers of households spending money. Thus, the two tables give the priorities for about two-thirds of the households. The range in the yearly expenditure per single household is wide, so that the last column gives the average expenditure per year.

Table 41. Priorities of expenditure items II

Items	Number of Households	Range in Shares per Year	Average Shares per Year
2. Fish	24	12-171	56
7. Spices	23	-/10-13	4
16. Maize flour	23	1-108	25
36. Household equipment	22	3-263	57
32. Chewing coffee	21	-/20-25	4
9. Sugar	21	-/40-174	15
27. Milk	20	-/50-165	10
44. Medicine	20	-/80-257	44
6. Onions	19	-/10-11	2
20. Cooking oil	19	-/20-40	4
25. Local beer	19	-/30-336	48
47. Social contributions	19	-/25-95	22

Table 42 gives another order according to the average amount of money spent on the items, thus giving the general trends for peoples' demands when they consider the major posts in their budgets. For priority items 2-6, two-thirds of the farmers used less than 60/-shares per year. Only clothes took, on the average, a greater share of the budget.

Table 42. Priorities of expenditure items III

Priorities	Number of Households	Average Shares per Year
1. Clothes	25	100
2. Household equipment	22	57*
3. Fish	24	56
4. Meat	25	48
5. Local beer	19	48
6. Medicine	20	44

*Household equipment = all utensils for the kitchen, sacks, mattresses, bedding, blankets, and the like.

Source: Jorgen Rald and Karen Rald, *Rural Organization in Bukoba District, Tanzania* (Uppsala, Sweden: Scandinavian Institute for African Studies, 1975). Used with permission of the authors and the Scandinavian Institute for African Studies.

why. In reality, much income distribution data describe income averaging rather than income distribution.

Wealth and Social Values

In traditional rural communities the following have been recognized as forms of wealth: livestock, vegetables, produce, nuts, timber, magical spells to produce fertility in gardens, ivory and animal teeth generally, shells, cloth and trade goods, and salt. These forms of wealth are not general media of exchange; rather, specific forms of wealth may only be used in particular social transactions. For example, ivory might only be used for bride price, while vegetables might only be used to purchase timber. The use of various wealth forms must be understood in their local setting. In many rural areas, money has limited functions, such as for payment of licenses, taxes, or bride price (see Table 3.2 for an example of expenditure patterns).

In traditional agricultural communities, a man's reputation may be the most valuable thing he possesses. Status may be much more important than possession of wealth forms or money income—prestige and admiration may be ranked above material goods. The results often seem odd to the outsider but they have an internal logic and consistency when the social context is grasped. Such values may affect the success of development projects, as in the following example:

> Traditional wealth forms are often preferred to money. Geoffrey Masefield recalls that as a young and inexperienced agricultural officer in Uganda, newly-posted to a remote district among an unfamiliar tribe, [he] was instructed by the Government to open the first agricultural experiment station in the district, and was provided with money to purchase, among other things, the best local cattle he could find for a foundation herd with which to practice selective breeding. [He] bought some young bulls without difficulty, but then found that, such was the social prestige attached to owning numbers of cattle, no stockowner in the district would sell any female animals capable of producing offspring, much less the best ones. Eventually [he] acquired a herd of which half the female animals had to be bought outside the district and were therefore unacclimatized, and the remainder were stunted, maimed, or thought by their owners to be barren—hardly a good start for what was intended to be a model herd to be further improved by selected breeding![12]

PATTERNS OF MOBILITY

Analysis of mobility patterns at the national level can aid conceptualization of extension arrangements to be included in the design of projects and, as with data on groups, where projects can be most advantageously located. For agriculture it may be necessary to consider not only human movement but also the distribution and siting of transport, credit, and marketing components. For a population project such considerations as location and overall geographic coverage of medical stations would be important in estimating the number of people likely to be affected by the project.

Patterns of movement at the national level can be broken down by significant participant activity (agricultural, trade, or religious, and the like) so that the most frequented place of personal contact (with opinion leaders, especially) could be identified.[13] Where seasonal activities are involved, the time of the year and the length of time involved can be of assistance. Fishing or harvesting activities are often seasonal; so, too, may be employment provided by tourism. If project extension activities aim to involve as many people as possible, then project managers must consider such seasonal migratory factors.

In West Africa, for example, over large areas all farmers live in villages ("nucleated settlements") from which they travel on foot or by bicycle to work their farms, though by no means every day and often only for a short time. In East Africa, by contrast, there are large areas in which every farmer lives in an isolated house on his own holding and where villages do not exist. The effects of these two systems on agricultural extension work are very different. In the West African case, it is rare that an extension worker can find the occupant of a bad farm actually working the land when he happens to pass by, and he is therefore denied the opportunity to discuss soils, crops, and animals on the spot; however, the village system makes it easy to gather together an audience of farmers for a talk or a demonstration. In East Africa, it is much easier to find the farmer on his farm because he lives there, but it is much more difficult to collect the scattered clients at a central point for a group session.

A similar obvious connection between social arrangements and extension work exists in the case of many grazing areas. Over most of Africa it is the custom that land not under crops or fenced is available to any local stockowner for grazing. It is impossible in these circumstances for the extension worker to advise any single individual to spend money or effort on the improvement of open pastures used by his stock by such measures as irrigation, drainage, or fertilizer use. If the individual does so, his neighbors' animals will move in and take advantage of the improved growth of grass and he will get a little reward for his effort. The extension worker therefore knows he has to affect group behavior or concentrate on getting pastures fenced before they will be improved.[14]

ACCESS TO BASIC HUMAN NEEDS

Who are the poorest, how numerous are they, and where are they located? What access to basic necessities do they now have? Indicating access is a process of showing the existing availability and utilization of the basic necessities required to sustain a minimum standard of living. Data should indicate the availability of income-earning opportunities, food and shelter, and services for education and health care, with particular reference to poor rural populations. Health care should not only include preventive and curative measures for characteristic diseases but also adequate supplies of potable water.[15]

Schools and hospitals are often sited near administrative centers whose locations were determined during the colonial period when concern was with the maintenance of law and order rather than with development. When assessing access and utilization data, it is necessary to make sure that the types of service offered are appropriate; for example, service by male medical technicians to Muslim women may not be acceptable. Counting effectiveness in terms of the number of doctors per thousand people, without knowing whether the usual kinds of health problems call for a doctor's skill—or if doctors will visit sick people living some distance away, or if the sick will visit the doctors— is not very helpful either. Likewise, estimating health care in terms of hospital beds, while sometimes useful is less so in cultures that consider illness a consequence of fate or that place a high value on caring for sick persons at home through use of traditional remedies.[16]

Data on provision of access and the extent of utilization are not enough. One must know the reasons for those figures. Utilization is best understood by finding out what the service offered means to the people concerned. Data may show that a large number of boarding schools may have been built with "x" capacity. But such schools may be unpopular and underutilized. Boarding schools are often used to achieve rapid change in pupils by taking them away from what educators feel to be the diluting influence of their "uneducated" parents. Perhaps the school system is too closely tied to one religious denomination. Perhaps the school system concentrates on one ethnic or tribal group by using their language, making other groups unwilling to attend.

AN ANALYTICAL DESCRIPTION OF THE POOR

As shown in Chapter 2, it is extremely dangerous to assume that creation of access to benefits will solve the problems of the poorest. A solution to human needs must rely on a knowledge of cultural resources. Poverty is not merely a matter of not having things or access to them; it is also a matter of how people behave in particular cultural contexts.

Unless analysis of the nature and causes of poverty takes place, fundamental misconceptions about why people are poor will persist. It used to be a common accusation by the British that the Malays of Malaya were "lazy" farmers uninterested in improvement, contrasting unfavorably in this respect with immigrant Malay farmers from Indonesia. Only a knowledge of Malay history enables one to realize that the Malays of Malaya do not primarily regard themselves as farmers at all. By tradition and preference they are seafarers (often making their living by piracy in the past) and fishermen. Farming was a distasteful secondary occupation, left largely to women and occasional idle hours.

There is no easy definition of poverty at the national level. In one area poverty may be a consequence of a lack of jobs or opportunities to make money, in another area it may be the result of landlessness and the introduction of sophisticated methods of agricultural production. Averages, such as average income or average caloric intake, can be misleading, since the target population is often below average.

TESTING THE DEFINITION

Regardless of whether social scientists or civil servants have undertaken sophisticated professional data collection or have personally produced maps and analyses on the basis of data already on record, they can test the adequacy of the inventory by considering the following questions.

Are comprehensive quantitative definitions of basic needs for the poorest people available? Are the places where the poorest people live known? Such definitions would comprehend income, literacy rates, morbidity and mortality figures, nutritional status, and so on. In a country with great geographical and social diversity it is unlikely that one quantitative definition of poverty, no matter how comprehensive, will suffice. These definitions should, as applicable, show the education, food, shelter and clothing, medical, and monetary requirements for raising people up to a nationally acceptable minimum standard.

Are comprehensive qualitative definitions of poverty available? Is there a significant difference between official quantitative definitions of basic needs and the subjective qualitative definition that people have of their own circumstances? For example, do poor people themselves believe that they are poor, uneducated, malnourished, and unhealthy, and do they want to make the kinds of changes that are implied by projects?

Why do the poorest remain poor? What are the behavioral reasons for their poverty? Do they lack skills in agriculture? Are organization and management capability weak? Is an absence of literacy the root cause of their condition in life? Is ignorance a problem? Is fatalism responsible for maintaining poverty? Are hunters and gatherers in tropical rain forests or desert pastoralists so attached to their way of life that they do not want to participate in wage labor or cash cropping? Alternatively, is it the behavior of the rich that must be changed? Whatever the causes and reasons, an inventory must analyze at the national level

MAP 3.3

Identification of Social Groups

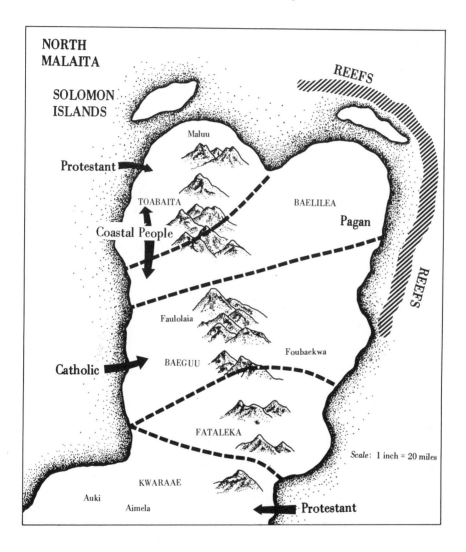

Note: Identification of social groups who have distinct languages, religious beliefs, or location makes it impossible for them to be merged with other groups. Each group here has a distinctly different language or dialect. The actual extent of social mapping is determined by the size of area to be affected directly or indirectly by projects.

Source: Compiled by the author.

MAP 3.4

Social Organization

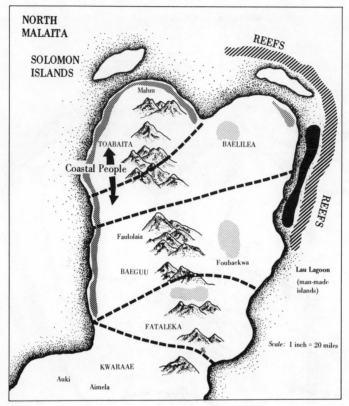

Note: Social organization is as follows: people in all areas live in villages, seldom larger than 300-400 in population. The total population in the above map is approximately 25,000. Property is held by groups of related males. Land tenure is individualized along the northwest coastal strip and inland for one to two miles. Social organization is on a clan basis in both pagan and Christian areas, with descent being traced to a common ancestor from whom all property rights emanate. None of the groups is very hierarchical. Leadership is based on demonstrated leadership capacity and is egalitarian in nature. The leaders, called "Big Men," initiate and execute agricultural as well as ritual activities. Everyone has access to land. Diet consists of tubers, fish, and coconuts.

There are three forms of wealth that are considered important: in the highest density population group, important wealth is thought to be radios, clothing, bicycles, firearms, and the like; in the second highest population density group, money is considered the most important wealth form; and in the least densely populated area, important wealth consists of pigs, tusks, and small highly polished pieces of shell threaded on string. In the latter group, land purchases and payment of bride price are transacted with shell wealth. The need for money is comparatively limited and inelastic.

Source: Compiled by the author

MAP 3.5

Mobility Patterns

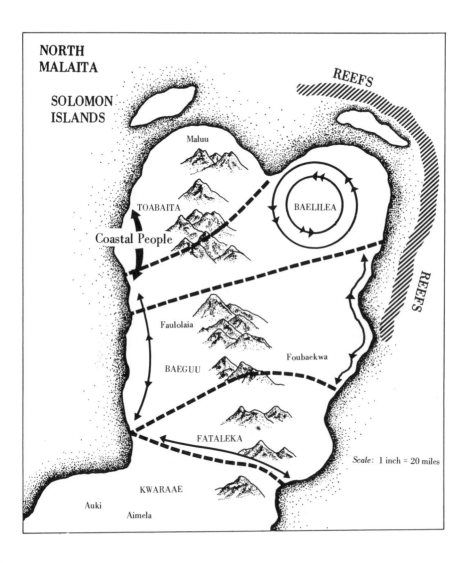

Note: Mobility patterns indicate that each of the groups has little contact with the other. This is due, in part, to the topography and to the differing cultural patterns. These data are important for decisions on the locations of projects and for assessments as to how projects may affect populations.

Source: Compiled by the author.

MAP 3.6

Nature and Location of Poverty

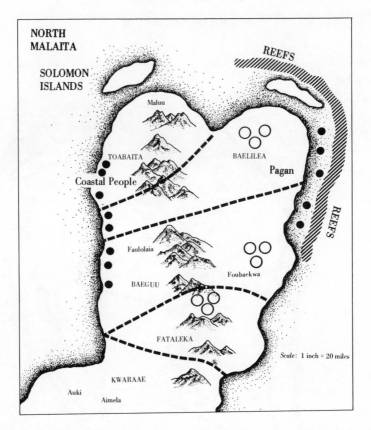

Legend:

● Poverty among this group (estimated at 10 percent of the total population in the area, that is, 9,000-15,000 persons per square mile) has increased because of the rising population pressure for the scarce coastal lands. The birthrate is 40 per 1,000. A recent trend is that good garden land is being used for copra and cocoa production; remaining garden lands have declining fertility. The traditional social system is breaking down as individualism grows. The poor are those who are landless or who are old and alone, as a consequence of their "modern" children having abandoned them. Among this group the lack of garden land has had serious nutritional consequences. A major problem is that a vigorous and successful agricultural extension program is actually contributing to poverty because more and more valuable garden land is being converted to cash crops. Another problem is that the position of women has deteriorated; traditionally, they had done most of the agricultural work, but government extension is male dominated.

○ Poverty among this group (estimated at 10 percent, or 5-10 persons per square mile) has increased because there is a lack of opportunity to engage in cash cropping (coconuts will not grow at such high altitudes and communications are very difficult). Nutritional status is very low. Poor roads have meant that there has been little governmental contact. However, group sentiments and traditional forms of social organization are still strong. Illiteracy is very high. A major problem is that increasing incomes, a consequence of road construction opportunities, have not helped the nutritional status of the people because monies have been gambled and used to purchase high prestige items such as shotguns, radios, and bicycles.

Source: Compiled by the author.

MAP 3.7

Implications of Social Mapping

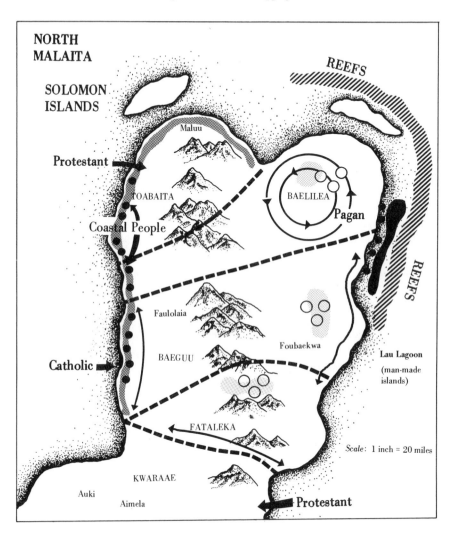

Note: Since there are different types of poverty with different causes and different impacts, the same type of project will not be useful in all areas where dire poverty is located. Because the poor have been located and identified, it is possible to see where projects should be located and to make a rough kind of assessment of their potential impact on poverty (see Figure 4.2). This mapping can help provide the essential linkage between the project and the area or regional plan. It is possible to estimate roughly how many projects must be mounted to give impact to a regional or national plan.

Source: Compiled by the author.

the behavioral roots of poverty. Unless projects reflect the fruits of such analysis, scarce resources will be wasted.

Is there discernible linkage between projects and the achievement of regional or national goals? Information from mapping should provide guidance not only on where projects can be most advantageous and what size those projects should be; it should also provide insight into the number of projects required in particular locations in order to effect a regional or national plan (see Maps 3.3-3.7).

RESERVATIONS ABOUT A "BASIC NEEDS" POLICY

Although the philosophical and humanistic content of a "basic needs" policy is attractive, there is legitimate apprehension about the effects of such a policy on attempts to improve and institutionalize the cultural appraisal of projects. Basic needs is successor to a number of earlier policies whose main defect was that they supposed that all problems were similar and that solutions were always possible, while obstacles were due to idiosyncratic cultural beliefs, values, and institutions. Those who devise policy, who plan and execute projects, and who give advice only begin to be useful when they recognize that they themselves may be part of the problem. Human dignity and culturally inspired self-expression remain the most basic need and are not necessarily assuaged by the kinds of basic needs program that are now often discussed.

Basic needs policies may fall into disrepute unless there is a clear statement about who can be helped and who cannot. Cultural appraisal procedures do not indicate who must be helped—those kinds of decisions usually depend on the exercise of political or economic judgment. However, no matter who the project beneficiaries are to be, one cannot forget that it is critically important to attend to the need to secure increases in productivity. While a concern that the benefits of growth be distributed equitably is to be remembered, one must also not lose sight of the fact that some kind of economic growth must be achieved if an increasing number of people are to be helped.

NOTES

1. See United Nations, Economic and Social Council, *Fifth Report on Progress in Land Reform*, 46th sess., agenda item 6 (February 24, 1969); Peter M. Raup, "Land Reform and Agricultural Development," in *Agricultural Development and Economic Growth*, ed. Herman McDowell Southworth and Bruce F. Johnston (Ithaca, N.Y.: Cornell University Press, 1967); Folke Corring, *Economic Results of Land Reforms* (Washington, D.C.: AID, 1970); *Spring Review of Agricultural Credit* (Washington, D.C.: AID, 1974), this was a paper on AID's findings and implications that pointed to a need for new agency manpower with skills in land tenure questions.

2. This and several other examples are given in Ernest McLeod Dowson and Vivian Lee Osborne Shepard, *Land Registration* (London: Her Majesty's Stationery Office, 1957).

3. See, for example, Milton J. Esman, *Administration and Development in Malaysia: Institution Building and Reform in a Plural Society* (Ithaca, N.Y.: Cornell University Press, 1972); Fred W. Riggs, *Administration in Developing Countries* (Boston: Houghton Mifflin, 1964); Victor A. Thompson, *Bureaucracy and Innovation* (University: University of Alabama Press, 1969); Bernard B. Schaffer, "Comparisons, Administration and Development," *Political Studies* 19 (1971). This has been underscored many times in recent years. An interesting elaboration of the theme is given in Jan C. de Wilde et al., *Experience with Agricultural Development in Tropical Africa* (Baltimore: Johns Hopkins University Press, 1967).

4. John C. Wilkinson, "The Organization of the Falaj Irrigation System in Oman," Oxford University, School of Geography, research paper no. 10.

5. Scarlett Epstein, "The Ideal Marriage between the Micro View of the Anthropologist and the Macro View of the Economist," *Economic Development and Cultural Change* (October 1976).

6. Ron Crocombe, *Two Blades of Glass*, ed. Peter Worsley (Manchester: Manchester University Press, 1972).

7. Evelyn Kessler, *Women, An Anthropological View* (New York: Holt, Rinehart and Winston, 1977).

8. See Daniel Lerner, *The Passing of Traditional Society* (Glencoe, Ill.: Free Press, 1958); Lucian W. Pye, *Aspects of Political Development* (Boston: Little, Brown, 1966).

9. Douwe G. Jongmans and Henri J. M. Claessen, eds., *The Neglected Factor* (Amsterdam: Van Gorcum, 1974).

10. Benjamin D. Paul, ed., *Health, Culture and Community* (Chicago: Aldine, 1961). This book provides a number of examples.

11. Harold K. Schneider, *Economic Man: The Anthropology of Economics* (New York: The Free Press, 1974), gives a wealth of useful information.

12. Based on Geoffrey B. Masefield's paper, "Agricultural Extension Work and Anthropology," in *What We Can Do for Each Other*, ed. Glynn Cochrane (Amsterdam: B. R. Gruner, 1976).

13. Ronald G. Knapp, "Marketing and Social Patterns in Rural Taiwan," *Annals of the Association of American Geographers* 61, no. 1 (March 1971).

14. Masefield, "Agricultural Extension Work."

15. John McHale and Magda Cordell McHale, *Basic Human Needs* (New Brunswick, N.J.: Transaction Books, 1977). A report to the UN environment program, Paul Streeten, "The Distinctive Features of a Basic Needs Approach to Development," *International Development Review* 9, no. 3 (1977).

16. This rests on personal observation in South America. See also the entire issue of *Journal of Development Studies* 8, no. 3, ed. Nancy Baster (July 1972), on the use of social indicators for poverty. This was also published as a book, *Measuring Development: The Role and Adequacy of Development Indicators* (London: F. Cass, 1972).

4 PROJECT DESIGN

Project managers, either personally or with professional assistance, who have the types of information outlined in Chapter 3 and who then address the criteria given here will increase the chances of having a project that is socially sound. As in the creation of an inventory of cultural resources, there are a number of criteria to be considered during project design, as follows:

Contextualism—assuring that the project ideas fit with the cultural landscape,
Incrementalism—assessing the magnitude of the social change involved,
Minimum participant profiles—analyzing the social characteristics of project participants,
Spread effects—estimating the magnitude of project impact,
Motivation—providing reasons for participation in projects,
Estimating time factors—approximating the length of time required for social change,
Benefit incidence—observing who gains and who loses during the life of a project,
Communication and learning—seeking ways of facilitating and encouraging innovation and adaptation,
Design of extension efforts—building the organization of extension work,
Using indigenous organization—maximizing the use of local management talent.

CONTEXTUALISM

The reason why construction of an inventory of cultural resources is important is because every development project must suit the prevailing social landscape or else resources may be wasted and popular confidence in development assistance efforts eroded. Agricultural innovations may require patterns of work

46

participation
~os +
r-p·

that are incompatible with local work patterns, while nutrition programs may rely on types of food that do not lend themselves to traditional methods of food preparation. The key factor in determining whether or not a project fits into a particular cultural milieu is participation. If participation calls for an abnormal response on the part of a project participant, the project will be inappropriate to the context and resources will be wasted.

Housing developments have often ignored the contextual principle, as in the following Indian example:

> The model for the new capital was New Delhi, with its broad streets of bungalows and open spaces in the British cantonment style. Since Bhubaneswar was to be Orissa's symbol of modernization and change, the cantonmentlike spaciousness was considered to be a desirable part of the sought-for higher standard of living. The fact that the dispersed settlement pattern made informal social gathering—especially for women who usually stayed close to home—very difficult; that the open spaces were impractical in a hot climate and hard to maintain; and that people had to go further to work or to market was less concern to the government than building a clean, modern-looking administrative center.[1]

Bhubaneswar house builders paid little attention to family living arrangements and a good deal of money was thereby wasted.

Organizational Contextualism

Papua New Guinea, for example, entertained a contextual proposal that entailed legal recognition of traditional tribes or lineages as corporate groups. Project staff from industrial countries, cooperatives, individual operations, and small businesses would usually consider laws and regulations to treat three distinct forms of organization in their context. For the creation of cooperatives, businesses, and land tenure entities, recognition of lineages requires rules and regulations for lineages to trade, hold real property, and sue or be sued. Replacing the traditional form of organization would require three new sets of legislation and three new sets of government workers.

In Liberia, attempts to import U.S.-style cooperatives failed while there was clearly an adequate indigenous organization that could perform functions associated with cooperatives in industrial countries. Use of a traditional organization, such as a lineage, can often maximize existing knowledge, patterns of leadership, and entrepreneurial skill.[2]

Many rural people are confused by a profusion of health, educational, agricultural, or cooperative extension workers, all concerned primarily with the fur-

therance of their own department's interests. These individuals are usually un-
aware of their collective impact at the village level. The level of structural specialization in rural development organizations should, as far as possible, be determined by the social and economic organization of the potential project participants and not the degree of specialization thought necessary for the most efficient dispatch of government business by the project planners. In other words, a
contextual approach is in order.

In 1971 an industrialist in Birmingham, England was exporting 115 different varieties of garden hoe. He related his output to physique, soil type, preference, and so on—an early example of appropriate technology. Attempts to introduce Indian plows to parts of East Africa failed both because the soils and topography were different from those in India and because the average Indian
zebu cow weighs around 800 pounds, while the average zebu in East Africa
weighs 400 pounds.

Ideological Contextualism

E. F. Schumacher gave an excellent example of ideological contextualism
in his treatment of Buddhist economics:

> While the materialist is mainly interested in goods, the Buddhist is
> mainly interested in liberation. But Buddhism is "The Middle Way"
> and therefore in no way antagonistic to physical well-being. It is not
> wealth that stands in the way of liberation but the attachment to
> wealth; not the enjoyment of pleasurable things but the craving for
> them. The keynote of Buddhist economics, therefore, is simplicity
> and non-violence. From an economist's point of view, the marvel of
> the Buddhist way of life is the utter rationality of its pattern—amaz-
> ingly small means leading to extraordinarily satisfactory results.
>
> For the modern economist this is very difficult to understand. He
> is used to measuring the "standard of living" by the amount of an-
> nual consumption, assuming all the time that a man who consumes
> more is "better off" than a man who consumes less. A Buddhist
> economist would consider this approach excessively irrational: since
> consumption is merely a means to human well-being, the aim should
> be to obtain the maximum of well-being with the minimum of con-
> sumption. Thus, if the purpose of clothing is a certain amount of
> temperature comfort and an attractive appearance, the task is to at-
> tain this purpose with the smallest possible effort, that is, with the
> smallest annual destruction of cloth and with the help of designs
> that involve the smallest possible input of toil.[3]

INCREMENTAL CRITERIA

Projects often fail because they try to produce too much change. Successful introduction of the kinds of social change represented by development projects calls for the least amount of social disruption consistent with the attainment of development objectives—an incremental approach is useful in this regard. Whether one is considering machinery, a systematic way of bookkeeping or accounting, or the use of fertilizer, it is necessary to examine the extent to which the kinds of social change the project calls for are incremental. John Turner and Robert Fichter discuss the need for incrementalism in regard to housing:

> A house is typically an indivisible product. Because of its complexity and the fact that it is attached to a particular piece of ground, it is removed from the effective demand of vast numbers of people who nevertheless have the need and the desire to become homeowners. And even for those who can buy this peculiarly expensive product, its complex subsystems often require the homeowner to become dependent on extremely expensive labor specialists.
>
> The imperative here is conspicuous: if home ownership (and this includes cooperative ownership of apartment-type structures) is to be extended to the many families presently excluded from the market, the components which make up a dwelling must be made simpler, must be made cheaper, and must be made in such a way that they can be assembled incrementally.[4]

Contextual Technology

Failure to ensure that planned changes are of an incremental nature will often lead to waste:

> Site and service programs are publicly sponsored subdivisions providing building lots and (generally minimum) services or utilities for low-income owner-builders. . . . there is a discernible trend away from publicly sponsored low-income housing projects in low-income countries. This is partly because they have proven to be so costly to the public (the loss of 60 percent or more of the funds invested through the beneficiaries' failure to repay loans is common) and partly because of the far greater effective demand for land without dwelling units (which most low-income people prefer to build themselves anyway).[5]

Incremental Benefits

Income for project participants should be incremental. It is not enough to simply assume adequate income levels; rather, one must understand the financial and cash flow needs of the poorest—what payments, social demands, ritual obligations, and so on are important. Levels of income should be adjusted to the financial needs of potential participants.

The use of incremental criteria can also enable project designers to calculate an appropriate scale of assistance for participants. It often seems that every small farmer is to have ten hectares in a resettlement project. Why ten? If too much assistance is given, then the project may succeed; though in other important respects, such as potential for spread or replication, the project may be unsuccessful. Costs of spread or replication are often too great, and so the benefits of such projects are not experienced outside the project area.

An example of a nonincremental approach comes from a project to produce palm oil in New Britain. Settlers' incomes were projected at about $A 1,000 per annum. Actual incomes of settlers turned out to be $A 2,000. People living outside the project area had annual incomes of less than $A 100 per annum. They became antagonistic toward the project participants. The project was an economic success and a social failure.

MINIMUM PARTICIPANT PROFILE CRITERIA

Project managers who know that people are poor and motivated to participate must make explicit to them the requirements of participation. What behavioral changes must occur among participants? If the very poor already possessed the skills, attitudes, beliefs, and material resources economic development requires, then many projects would not be necessary. When a project manager believes a project is necessary, a thorough description of what resources participants have or do not have is an important step in confirming the soundness of the design calculations.

What Do Participants Need?

A profile of the potential participants should be constructed to specify the minimum resource requirements. For example, what sex, level of education, resources, skills, and attitudes will make individual participation possible? Is the project designed for men and women of a particular socioeconomic status or religious persuasion? For agricultural production projects, being able to read fertilizer labels may be important; for marketing projects, numeracy may be important. With all projects, some change is required. Is diligence, or patience, or perseverance important? Each project demands that participants possess certain kinds of skills and attributes. These assumptions about the average participant must be made explicit.

Is It the Right Target Group?

If a project is to be properly designed, then the minimum participant profile should be based on the attributes and resource requirements that characterize the poorest in the inventory of cultural resources and human needs. It is then possible to see who should participate, considering the location and type of group with which a particular type of project could achieve maximum effect. It should then also be possible to identify those who cannot be expected to participate.

SPREAD EFFECT CRITERIA

Spread effects develop when the kinds of innovation introduced spread to areas beyond the project location. Replication is the process of executing a project in the same way in a new location. Obviously, spread effects are more desirable. Since project resources may be too scarce to allow for every poor person's becoming a direct recipient of self-help aid, the diffusion of effects beyond the initial population is a critical issue in project design.[6] An example of spread effect evaluation is shown in Figure 4.1. Problems to be considered involve characteristics of participants, replicability, conformity to the principles of contextualism and incrementalism, as well as project location (see Figure 4.2).

Spread Design Focus

If spread effects are to occur, projects must be designed with the characteristics of the poorest in mind—the poorest are those who are to be helped. If the poorest can successfully participate with the help of project resources, the well-off should have a chance to emulate their performance without as many project resources. Reversing this situation would seem to preclude the possibility of the poorest being helped. This logic reinforces the need for a minimum participant profile.

Anticipating Replication

Project design must pay attention to replicability.[7] For example, an oil palm project in New Guinea easily exceeded its projected rate of return, produc-

FIGURE 4.1

Calculating the Spread Effects of New Dairy Farming

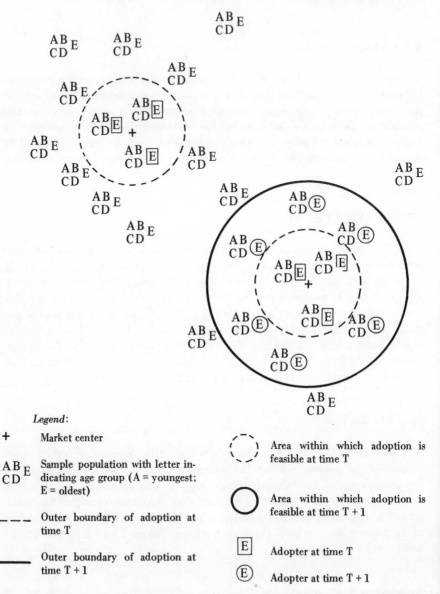

Legend:

+   Market center

AB E / CD   Sample population with letter indicating age group (A = youngest; E = oldest)

- - -   Outer boundary of adoption at time T

———   Outer boundary of adoption at time T + 1

Area within which adoption is feasible at time T

Area within which adoption is feasible at time T + 1

E   Adopter at time T

E   Adopter at time T + 1

Source: "Innovation Diffusion in a Developing Economy," *Economic Development and Cultural Change*, vol. 21, January 1973. Used with permission of the author and *Economic Development and Cultural Change*.

FIGURE 4.2

Project Identification

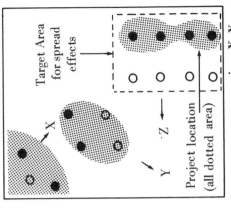

A. **Location of participants—8 of 15 fit profile**

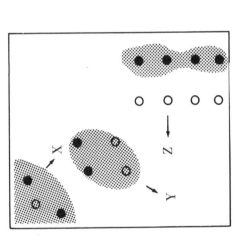

B. **Mobility pattern**

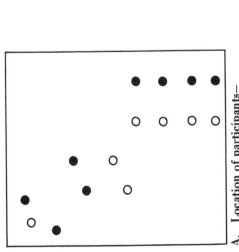

C. **Project location, given X, Y, and Z— Z has maximum impact**

○ Poorest in project area

● Poorest who fit minimum participant profile

Note: For an example of social mapping data on which such calculations are based see map 3.3.

Source: Compiled by the author.

ing very high incomes for farmers. But investment costs of approximately $15,000 per settler were much too high for the government to replicate this substantially. Further, it would have been impossible for the government to obtain the necessary land.

Poor design, that which is neither incremental nor contextual, can lessen the chances for achievement of spread effects. For example, in a project to improve the management of Spanish ports, new systems of financial accounting were introduced. The port authority was staffed by personnel with long-term appointments in the national civil service. Financial innovation did not really succeed because the accounting staff, on limited tours of duty with the port authority, perceived that their promotion, in the long run, depended on performance in terms of national civil service criteria, not in terms of port authority accounting practices.

Spread can, of course, sometimes occur for reasons having nothing to do with a project. In a series of projects to improve Uruguayan livestock, three socioeconomic levels could be distinguished—the very poor, the middle class, and the very wealthy ranchers. Neither the very rich nor the very poor took advantage of the projects. With extreme price fluctuations for meat, the poorest could not risk participation, since failure might imperil family livelihood. The rich did not need additional income. The middle class had to participate merely to maintain their position.

MOTIVATION CRITERIA

Motivation criteria can help tailor resources to project needs. Too often project designers assume that their appreciation of projects will be shared by project participants. Yet, each group of individuals expected to participate must be motivated—the actual motivation of the group, not that of a designer from outside that group, must be utilized. As in industrialized countries, some may be motivated by a desire for increased power and prestige, others may desire to follow the example of opinion leaders, others may seek financial reward, and still others may be moved by patriotism due to the key role a project may play in the nation's economy. Careful assessment of motivation can avert wasting of project resources. Extension budgets need not be high when participants are highly motivated.

It must not be assumed that all motivations are conducive to development as the planners perceive it.[8] Motivation is twofold, comprehending both the incentive or perception needed to make a given population interested in a project and the population's perception of the probable gains from the project. In Turkey a printing press with modern machinery failed even though there were many orders due to motivation factors. The managers did not like to take large orders that would take up all their working time, since they then were unable to fill small orders from their friends for wedding invitations and so on.

An assessment of perceived need is important because it points to the kinds of extension work that may be necessary. A health project will usually require much more explanation than a road. If people perceive a need for an innovation or change, then chances for adoption without significant resources being devoted to extension work are good. For example, when able-bodied males left their villages to work in Zambian copper mines, those who remained at home wanted to learn to write so that they could communicate with the migrants—education projects succeeded.

By assessing the degree of risk from a potential participant's viewpoint, project managers can estimate the likelihood of participation. New seeds and plant types will often be adopted if they can first be tested, but most farmers are unwilling to commit all their resources to an unknown innovation. This is true of farmers all over the world, since failure threatens family security and well-being. Can the innovation or change be broken down into small or simple tasks? Can a small amount of a new crop be planted to see how well it does? One cannot assume a desire on the part of participants for profit maximization or cost minimization without supporting evidence; increased income may not be welcome if it obligates participants to support a whole new wave of relatives, for example. It should be possible for individuals or groups to participate without incurring a heavy penalty. For example, those who have increased incomes must be able to continue to discharge their traditional social obligations.

ESTIMATING TIME FACTORS

Every project is an experiement in social change. Sound project design requires an assessment of time required for new kinds of behavior to become so well established that they will survive and spread after the withdrawal of externally provided project resources. If participants learn how to grow coffee from expatriate advisers teaching new methods and techniques, will they continue to care for the trees in the same manner after the advisers have left? In projects to train teachers of English as a second language, the same question arises: Will it continue after the experts have gone?

Termination of Resources and Social Change

It is necessary to distinguish two dates—the date on which all project assistance will cease to be delivered and the date by which social change will have been achieved. For example, clinics to improve nutrition may be constructed and all personnel trained within two years, but the behavioral change in the population in response to the provision of these project inputs may take four to five years. Education projects may not achieve social change for five to ten years;

livestoek improvement projects may last for five years, although changes in animal husbandry may take from 10 to 15 years; family planning programs may last for three years, although reproductive behavior may only change after a decade. If contextual and incremental principles have been followed, there should already be some individuals who have successfully adopted the innovation. Time estimates in the project should reflect the fruits of this experience.

Time as a Test of Feasibility

Time allocation by males and females, including seasonal variations, must be evaluated (see Figure 4.3).[9] A livestock improvement project in Papua New Guinea encountered difficulties when designers of the project decided that twice as much pig food, and higher incomes, could be produced if farmers gave up their "leisure time"; however, the activities to be abandoned for fulfillment of this plan were more highly valued than pig food production, thus Melanesians rejected one of the fundamental assumptions underlying the project. Adult literacy programs in some rural villages in Ghana failed because it was not realized that between June and December many young Ghanians were fishing or working on cocoa farms. Similarly, tourist resorts that rely on labor from surrounding rural areas should relate their needs to seasonal agricultural labor requirements.

Simple recording of time spent in the fields by various family members is inadequate, since their presence in the fields may only be possible as a result of the work of other family members. What must be estimated is the total allocation of family labor throughout the year. What effect do age, sex, or family seniority have on the allocation of family labor? Are there significant differences between families with high productivity and those with low productivity? What kinds of labor are most highly valued and which are least valued?

In addition to family labor and individual performance, it is important to record occasions that call for village work forces or the combined labor of a number of families. Such occasions are the construction of new houses or storage facilities and the initial clearing of new ground. These data will be of great value in project design, since projects should, as far as possible, take cognizance of existing work patterns and their time implications.

BENEFIT INCIDENCE

Increasing concern with benefiting poor groups that were largely bypassed by earlier development processes creates a special need to identify the social impact of a project.[10] The best opportunity to do this is at the initial stage of project conception and formulation, when it is still possible to reject a project if its social impact is regressive, to modify it to make it more compatible with equity

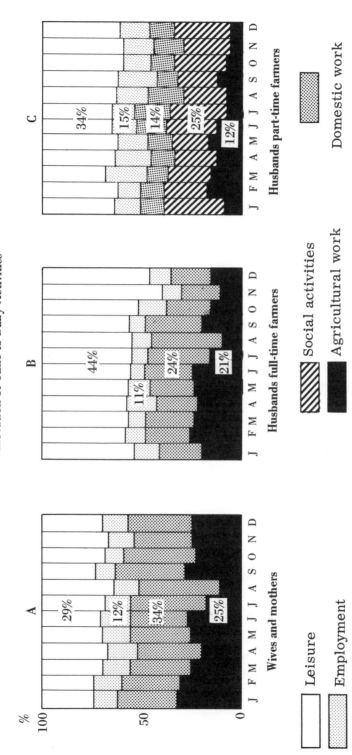

FIGURE 4.3

Allocation of Time to Daily Activities

A — Wives and mothers

B — Husbands full-time farmers

C — Husbands part-time farmers

Leisure

Employment

Social activities

Agricultural work

Domestic work

Source: Jorgen Rald and Karen Rald, *Rural Organization in Bukoba District, Tanzania* (Uppsala, Sweden: Scandinavian Institute for African Studies, 1975). Used with permission of the authors and the Scandinavian Institute for African Studies.

objectives, or to consider appropriate compensatory measures to rectify the damage or losses to those who are likely to be adversely affected. It is important that the groups the project is intended to help, those who are likely to be adversely affected, and those who may be indirectly affected, either positively or negatively (for example, ultimate consumers of a basic product, the price of which is reduced or increased), be identified at an early stage.

In assessing benefit incidence, one must bear in mind that the recipient of the goods or services provided under a project is not necessarily the person to whom the major benefits of the project accrue. A tenant farmer, for instance, may receive new seeds, fertilizer, and credit to pay for them, thus raising his yield, yet the landlord may raise the rent and so appropriate the lion's share of the incremental income flow. In order to continue to hire the land at the new (higher) rent the tenant farmer must continue his new practices, but this may involve much more labor on his part and perhaps greater risk. How much benefit does he get?

Identifying the incidence of benefits is similar to identifying those who bear the burden of indirect taxes—both are affected by how much of the benefit or cost is passed on. Assessment of the distribution of benefits and costs utilizes data and insights obtained about the project population in connection with the study of the sociocultural feasibility of the plan. In considering equity and benefit incidence, a limited number of criteria—access to resources and opportunities; employment situation; rural displacement, migration, and urbanization; and changes in power and participation—seem especially important for assessing the social costs and benefits of projects.

Access to Resources and Opportunities

Access to land, capital, credit, education, health, nutrition services, and markets, and the ways and extent to which such access is broadened or narrowed, must be assessed. The issues to be identified and analyzed under this heading include, in the case of an agricultural loan, for example, trends in land tenure arrangements and how they would be affected; the availability to target farmers of improved inputs (seeds and fertilizers), implements, and the credit with which to finance them; access to technical information and to markets, including the existence and extent of farm-to-market roads; and how price policy, including taxes and subsidies, affects the target group. Such criteria measure the potential effect of the project on the distribution of wealth and income.

Measurement of access is more useful than measurement of money incomes alone, since the very poor do not always use money. Poor people with low money incomes might be quite satisfied with their lot and with the level of government services; those with high money incomes might be completely unsatisfied with government services, such as health and education. Recent experience in parts of rural Mexico has shown that standards of nutrition may even decline as income increases.

Using the criteria developed for the national inventory of cultural resources and project designs the number of persons with access to basic necessities prior to the project can be estimated together with changes in the nature of access and numbers of those having access due to the project. It should be possible to estimate how many more people will have new or improved access to health, nutrition, and education as a result of a project. It should also be possible, using the criteria developed, to demonstrate the demographic and socioeconomic implications of the new access distribution.

Employment

Among the issues to be in an assessment of employment benefits are factor intensity and the related question of the amount and type of employment to be generated or eliminated as a result of the project. Employment may be part-time, employing people whose major effort is in agriculture in locally situated light industry and fitting into agricultural slack periods. It is especially important to consider and predict the implications for target groups characterized by serious unemployment or underemployment, such as both rural and urban unskilled workers and the educated unemployed.

Employment policies, besides being directed toward males, are associated with the money-using sector. Employment is created and sustained in this sector. Thus, a choice of life-styles appropriate to the monetized sector is forced upon those wishing to receive government assistance.[11] This contrast between sectors is also encouraged by the fact that measurements of development, or lack of the same, are in terms of the money-using sector: success becomes the degree to which the money-using sector can encroach on the other sector. Instead of concentrating on creation of wage-earning jobs, there are many instances in which efforts should be concentrated on achieving productive increases in the subsistence sector.

Rural Displacement, Migration, and Urbanization

What groups might be pushed off the land or otherwise uprooted as a result of the project, where would they likely move, and how would they be reabsorbed into the economic and social life of the country? Public works projects often uproot people. Since project participants are often middle- or upper-class, poor people sometimes must move if they are to survive.

Because contemporary rural development planning overemphasizes increases in agricultural production at the expense of the integrity of the rural social systems, economically sound projects often produce unintended and undesirable social consequences. For example, production could perhaps be increased among an African or Asian family working as a group to produce goods and services from family lands by individualizing tenure arrangements; however, those land tenure arrangements would be socially disruptive while group sentiments remained strong. The weak and unskilled would be forced off the land. Models of behavior encountered in rural education may lead rural pupils to seek an urban existence as a nurse, engineer, government clerk, or construction worker. Urban migration as a consequence of such education constitutes a social cost.

Changes in Power and Participation

Changes in power relationships and participation may take place among the target group and different socioeconomic, regional, ethnic, and other groupings. As each of the preceding criteria (access, employment, and displacement) is related to the redistribution of power and opportunities for participation, ways in which such shifts affect the capacity of different groups to influence public policy must be recognized.

Nigeria provides two typical instances of such issues, both concerning an important cash crop, the oil palm. Here the advice to plant oil palms of high-yield varieties, instead of collecting fruit from low-yield wild palms, was at first resisted by local chiefs on the ground that it would lead to claims of individual tenure of land and thus undermine tribal authority. A little later, the introduction of oil presses and of nut-cracking machines to obviate laborious manual methods of preparing oil and kernels was bitterly resisted by the women because they had previously done the manual work, earning useful cash that custom allowed them to keep for themselves. In the case of the chiefs, it would have been useful to involve them in discussions at the project design stage. The opposition of the women to the introduction of new machinery was probably inevitable and should have raised doubts as to whether the innovations were appropriate technology.

COMMUNICATION AND LEARNING

As every project is an educational project, project managers must articulate a pedagogical model that will highlight exactly learning needs of the project participants, how this learning is to take place, and how long the process should last. Communication with potential participants in the project and nearby areas is a priority issue in estimating spread effects. This is often complicated by the cultural distance between change agents and participants, especially when the latter are rural, poor, uneducated, and may belong to different ethnic, linguistic, or religious groups.[12]

Social Context of Learning

Some years ago short residential courses for practicing farmers were started by the agricultural extension service in Uganda. People to attend these courses were at first selected by extension officers on the basis of what appeared to be outstanding ability or interest. Such a process naturally collected individuals from different areas, usually not near neighbors. Follow-up soon after the courses revealed that most soon gave up using any improved methods that they had been taught and relapsed into using the methods practiced around them. It was diagnosed that three things were wrong: isolated individuals soon forgot much of the detail learned in the course, whereas a group with the opportunity to discuss it together might have had a better collective memory; isolated individuals attempting improvements not understood by those around them, and who often provoked scorn or hilarity, tended to lack the strength of mind to persist with them, whereas a neighborhood group might have provided moral support; and, in some parts of the country, control of land use was in the hands of the extended family, and a single, generally young, member of the family group could not alone make the changes required for improved methods.

After this diagnosis, a different policy was adopted, one of selecting course participants as neighborhood groups and, in relevant cases, as groups (usually of varied age and status) within extended families. It was found that although this method resulted in fewer individuals of outstanding character being selected the ultimate effects in farm improvement were greater than under the former policy.

In West Africa, an agricultural extension service urged farmers to give cropped land a periodic rest under planted grasses to restore fertility. When a few farmers began to adopt this method, a problem arose with these grassed areas because other farmers claimed that, under customary law, land not actually planted with crops was available to the community either for free grazing (which in this case usually meant overstocking and consequent erosion) or for reallocation to other farmers who wished actually to plant crops. A solution was eventually found when the extension workers discussed the matter with the tribal chiefs, who decided that they could interpret the customary law so that planted grass was deemed to be a crop and thereby given protection against encroachment.

Technology for Learning

Projects need an explicit statement on the learning model to be used and the strategy to be employed in conveying the message. Projects involve behavioral change. Decisions need to be taken as to whether participants' learning should be based on example, reading, or seeing.[13] How, for example, are illiterate peasants supposed to learn how to use condoms? A medical team was trying to enlist the cooperation of villagers in a malaria eradication project by showing movies of a greatly enlarged anopheles mosquito. The team got little cooperation because villagers, never having seen huge mosquitoes, did not think the program related to their needs.

Rather than assuming that all peasants should learn in the same way, an attempt must be made to find out how learning is best accomplished in a specific cultural milieu. Attempts in East Africa during World War II to encourage African enlistment in British armed forces tried to whip up martial enthusiasm by showing George VI reviewing the air force, the army, and the navy in three different uniforms on three different occasions. The advertisement drew little response from the intended audience because the idea of any man having three suits of clothes was not believable.[14] It was found in the South Pacific that assistant medical officers could promote cocoa growing better than could radio, posters, or contact with agricultural extension workers: assistant medical officers had much more status than agricultural assistants. Solomon Islanders watched the assistant medical officers when they went home on annual leave. When they saw them grow cocoa they did the same. Had the Agricultural Department taken advantage of this situation the results might have been interesting.

Successful communication requires a strategy—identification of points of origin and destination for communication, identification of roles of planners and participants, and the establishment of frequency of communication. News media links—for example, radio, newspapers, and personal contacts—have to be instituted. Decisions should be made on which media to use and on how to facilitate feedback so that necessary improvements can be made.

DESIGN OF EXTENSION EFFORTS

Relying on what has been learned from communications analysis, the composition of project teams can proceed. The sex, ethnic, religious, or linguistic background of project personnel should correlate with local learning needs. Special attention should be paid to estimating the social distance between project personnel and village people. Where social distance is considerable, extension efforts will have little impact on the behavior of potential project participants. For example, an extension worker in South America, anxious to demonstrate that he was an "educated person," much superior to "illiterate peasants," regularly arrived in the fields to talk to his clients wearing a pinstripe suit and a homburg hat.

Mobility Patterns

Extension design must take people's movements, seasonal or permanent, into account. Where do they go to work, to market, to shop, to look at demonstration farms, or for leisure? See Figure 4.4 for a comparative example of such patterning. Each group has a radius of mobility, or outer limit, beyond which there are few personal contacts.[15]

Mobility patterns for officials should be planned on the same basis, reflecting the maximum distance traveled from home stations, location of home stations and areas to be visited, activities, duration of contacts with clients, and frequency of such contacts. Since in planning agricultural extension work it is often difficult to reach village people working on their farms, evening visits may be the most useful. In a project to improve maternal health care in South Asia, fixed facilities were constructed to handle serious cases; however, since the most ill preferred to stay home by their fires, and the medical staff did not like to walk long distances through rough terrain, health care remained inadequate. If demonstration farms are to be visited by women, then the farms must be in close proximity to villages, since women with responsibilities for child care cannot travel far or be away from their homes for long periods.

Epidemiologists have made great use of mobility patterns. In the fight against smallpox in West Africa, an understanding of mobility patterns proved to be crucial in containing the spread of the disease. It was noticed that the disease spread less rapidly during the monsoon season when poor weather made travel difficult. With this knowledge, the most efficient way to contain and eradicate the disease could be planned.

Jobs and Training

Jobs should be designed with the contextual and incremental criteria in mind. Project managers should be careful about uncritical use of industrial country expertise and "know-how." Jobs of a particular historical type—teacher, lawyer, doctor, agronomist, and so on—are often the product of the unique experience and development of industrial countries. The appropriateness of training for these jobs often needs to be questioned. For example, in West and East Africa there are African barristers who follow British legal training and tradition. These barristers have, however, little knowledge and understanding of traditional African law and custom. It might have been better to try to design these African legal jobs to cover the totality of African legal experience. How can specialization be made congruent with the maximum utilization of indigenous management potential?

Training deemed necessary to promote the modernization process should be designed, in terms of its organizational concomitants, to mediate between the traditional and the modern. Instead of providing agricultural officers in developing countries with professional training primarily based on cash cropping and industrialized-country agriculture, they should be taught more about traditional agriculture in their own countries and how increases in productivity in the sub-

FIGURE 4.4

Mobility Patterns

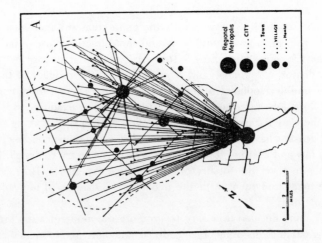

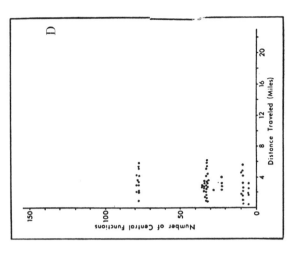

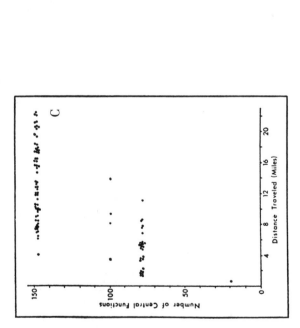

Note: A and B represent towns visited; C and D represent distances traveled for purchase of clothing and yard goods by C (the "modern" Canadian), and D (Old Order Mennonite populations of southwestern Ontario). The Mennonites wear simple homemade clothing and use the horse and buggy as the sole means of transportation. In contrast to the modern Canadians, they purchase all yard goods from nearby communities (compare C and D) and thus ignore the study area's hierarchy of central places based upon functional specialization. This is not true, however, for the use of banks, appliance outlets, and medical services, where the Mennonites behave like modern Canadians.

It is not always necessary to have highly sophisticated modeling of mobility. The important thing is to record significant countrywide mobility patterns that could offset project design and execution.

Source: Robert A. Murdie, "Cultural Differences in Consumer Travel," *Economic Geography* 41 (July 1965): 221, 231. Used with permission of the author and *Economic Geography.*

sistence sector might be achieved.[16] In this way, the unfortunate and unnecessary dichotomy between agricultural models emphasizing cash cropping and those emphasizing subsistence can be avoided.

Training is a fairly pragmatic process in the development business. Training programs convey a sense of agreement between donor and recipient about what is to be done.[17] Training, often depicted as the transfer of skills, is in some sense removed from the kind of debate that engulfs employment policies, income distribution, and so on. "Institution building" is thought to be accomplished by strengthening the middle management and reviewing the salary structures and promotion procedures. Types of training used by trainers combine to foster the idea that training is a universal problem in development, with a more or less universal set of responses.

It is not helpful, in a consideration of training, to make plans for the transfer of institutions or the transfer of resources. One cannot transfer institutions from one society to another: such an attempt represents an effort to graft ideas about institutionalized items of behavior that originated in one culture onto a situation that appears to have similar needs, although situated in another culture. For example, one could transfer the institution of marriage to a promiscuous society but there is no way to ensure its having the same meaning in its new setting that it had in its original setting.

Designing projects on the assumption that the process is one of a transfer of resources is also a mistake. When a physical training instructor gives muscle-building advice, the physical development of the pupil is not the result of a resource transfer. When a doctor cures or helps a patient he does not think of himself as transferring resources. Both pupil and patient play their part and determine the final course of things. The notions of "transfer" and "counterpart" are misleading in a training context because they downplay the most essential ingredient, the participant's contribution. It is, however, possible to identify practices that have been successful in diverse societies in the formation and operation of institutions.

USING INDIGENOUS ORGANIZATION

Project managers must decide on the basic organizational design for a project. This means deciding what existing organizational forms will be suitable and what kinds of adaptation may be necessary. A lack of management capability for local action can create a serious impediment to the success of rural development projects—which are fundamentally "people" and "community" oriented and the effective execution of which ultimately depends upon indigenous management. They not only elevate production levels, but attempt to do this in ways that serve distributive ends. However, attempts to improve management often do not work because over-trained people may be unwilling to do work not consistent with their level of training. It may be useful to experiment with innovative programs involving cycles of work and training over an extended period of time. In this fashion the desire for and desirability of higher levels of education can be aligned with practical requirements for carrying out the specific tasks of development activity.

Projects to promote rural development must be carried out in an extraordinarily complex social and economic framework.[18] Conceptualization of rural development has to start with an appropriate mode for production and distribution of goods and services. Later, health and nutrition measures must be linked to those productive and distributive activities. The kinds of education required to prepare for such a life must then be designed. The interactions and interdependencies of these complex elements make it highly unlikely that any alien organizational form will be highly successful.

The basic decision to be taken involves, initially, an assessment of the workability of the local institutions. There is nothing new about such decisions. British colonialism rested largely on its ability to work with and through local rulers—indirect rule. Indirect rule concentrated on social control rather than social change. Perfected by Lord Lugard in northern Nigeria, it meant governing in cooperation with local chiefly structures.[19] The problem with indirect rule was that it usually buttressed an archaic social system. It often strengthened the position of chiefs who had previously been tottering on their thrones. This government structure was suited to collecting taxes and having orders passed down, but it neither favored widespread local participation nor rewarded local development initiative. When colonial thinking swung in favor of social change, it did not always meet with success, partly due to a failure to realize that northern Nigeria had a social structure suited to indirect rule, and was thus very different from countries without central institutions and elaborate class hierarchies, such as Sierra Leone and Guyana. This situation has not changed. In some instances new institutions must be created; in others old institutions must be modified. In all instances the principles of contextualism and incrementalism must be applied. Organization design requires judgment; the exercise of judgment can be aided by the application of a number of criteria.

Organizational Charter

What is a local organization's charter? What range of things are forbidden and disallowed? For example, age-graded organizations made up of young men of a particular age in East Africa provide help and assistance to visiting grade cohorts; however, such organizations, if composed of men living within a wide geographical area, have limited potential value for projects requiring large-scale localized organization. The *compadrazgo* ritual kinship relationships of South America and the *slametan* mutual aid relationships in Indonesia are localized and personal and would not easily lend themselves to adaptation as project-specific forms of organization. Secret societies for males, Duk Duk of the New Hebrides or Poro of Liberia, are obviously dedicated to activities unhelpful to project work.

On the other hand, voluntary associations made up of Mexican urban migrants to the United States have organized projects ranging from provision of bars and clubs to hiring of teachers and arranging of health insurance. Lineage and clan organizations have, in addition to performing traditional kinship roles, operated stores, plantations, milling facilities—a whole host of entrepreneurial activities. Experience suggests that voluntary associations and traditional kinship groups have the kinds of charters that are most easily adapted to project organization.

More specialized forms of traditional organization may suggest their appropriateness because traditional and modern functions appear to be similar. Following this thinking, "barefoot doctors" have been given health roles and traditional priests have been given teacher roles. These attempts have seldom worked because the charter under which barefoot doctors and traditional priests work is not easily redefined to include modern functions. The functions may appear to be similar, but modern health and modern teaching are neither understood nor recognized within the beliefs that constitute the organizational charts.

Membership and Affiliation

It is important to assess the utility of organizations that are already widely representative. If such organizations are to become involved with a project, membership or affiliation ought to encompass both sexes and as many able-bodied adults as possible. Membership is usually not a card-carrying matter in rural areas, nor is it necessarily a fact of daily life. Kinship groups and voluntary associations usually have more flexible membership rules than religious associations. Many important organizational memberships are activated only when specific work tasks have to be accomplished or when seasonal harvesting is necessary. Considerable judgment is required to make these assessments and it is likely that project managers will seek professional guidance.

Functions and Leadership

The full range of functions performed by a traditional organization should be fully investigated. For the most part, rural organizations in the Third World are multipurpose, that is, they perform a wide range of functions consistent with their charters. Degree of technical skill, as revealed by task completion, literacy, and numeracy of organization members, should be covered by the investigation.

Project managers can then compare the results with project organizational requirements.

It is important to delineate the characteristics and functions of leadership in assessments of traditional organizations. Where individual choice is not circumscribed by social obligations or institutional regulations, it will be useful to know who opinion leaders are and where they are located. To what extent are they enthusiastic about the project? To what extent can their support be enlisted? Successful projects always need positive publicity.

CONCLUSIONS

Anticipation is the cardinal principle of project design. If future problems are recognized at the design stage, then implementation becomes easier. Stress on anticipation as a principle is all the more important because, hitherto, social science assistance has usually been sought after problems have arisen. While it is not possible, in the absence of a satisfactory theory of social change, to correctly forecast all eventualities, it is possible to design projects to minimize negative factors and to ensure that should negative factors intrude they can be speedily recognized. The criteria examined in the initial stages of project formulation assist in assessment of a particular project's prospects for success.

The only really valid assumptions in a discussion about project design are those for which data can be supplied. One cannot assume that opportunities provided for the poorest will be utilized by the poorest. Food can be made available, incomes can be raised, birth control materials can be made accessible, schools and hospitals can be constructed—project designers must assure that these will be advantageously used by the intended beneficiaries.

NOTES

1. John Turner and Robert Fichter, *Freedom to Build* (New York: Macmillan, 1972), p. 102.

2. Henry D. Seibel and Simon A. Massing, *Traditional Organizations and Economic Development: Studies of Indigenous Cooperatives in Liberia* (New York: Praeger, 1974). This study shows that it is more efficient to try to improve indigenous organizations than to import alien organizational types.

3. Ernest Schumacher, *Small Is Beautiful: Economics as if People Mattered* (New York: Harper & Row, 1964), p. 59.

4. Turner and Fichter, *Freedom to Build*, p. 276.

5. Ibid., p. 157.

6. Michael J. Rodell, "Growth Centers—Two Recent Contributions," *Economic Development and Cultural Change* 23, no. 3 (April 1975); Raanan Weitz, "Spatial Organization of Rural Development," in the undated publication no. 3 of the Settlement Study Center, Rehovet, Israel.

7. Lawrence A. Brown, "Diffusion of Innovation, a Macro View," *Economic Development and Cultural Change* 17, no. 2 (1969).

8. There is a wealth of anthropological data on this. See, for example, Charles Erasmus, *Man Takes Control* (Minneapolis: University of Minnesota Press, 1961). In my *Big Men and Cargo Cults* (Oxford: Clarendon Press, 1970), I showed that a desire among Melanesians to participate in millenarian activities had a beneficial impact on the government's efforts to further development.

9. See Peter Savage, *Of Time and Change: Temporal Perspectives in Development Administration*, Comparative Administration Group Paper (Bloomington, Ind.: Indiana University, 1965). For an account of how one anthropologist used time as a measuring rod to assess economic activity in traditional society, see Richard Salisbury, *From Stone to Steel* (Melbourne, Australia: Melbourne University Press, 1962).

10. Edward Spicer, *Human Problems in Technological Change* (New York: Russell Sage Foundation, 1965), gives numerous examples.

11. See Keith Hart, "Informal Income Opportunities and Urban Employment in Ghana," *Journal of Modern African Studies* 2, no. 1 (1973); Eugene Staley and Richard Morse, *Modern Small Industry for Developing Countries* (New York: McGraw-Hill, 1965); John Weeks, "Does Employment Matter," *Manpower and Unemployment Research in Africa* 4, no. 1 (April 1971). See Dharmar Kumar, "Technical Change and Dualism within Agriculture in India," *Journal of Development Studies* 7, no. 1 (1970); Hla Myint, *Dualism and the Internal Integration of Development* (Milan, Italy: Banco Nazionale del Lavoro, June 1970).

12. See, for example, Daniel Lerner and Wilbur Schramm, eds., *Communication and Change in the Developing Countries* (Honolulu: East-West Center, 1967).

13. See, for example, Marshall H. Segall, Donald T. Campbell, and Melville J. Herskovits, *The Influence of Culture on Visual Perception* (Indianapolis: Bobbs Merrill, 1965).

14. This, and other examples, are to be found in Leonard W. Doob, *Communication in Africa* (New Haven, Conn.: Yale University Press, 1961).

15. Murray Chapman, "Geography and the Study of Development," *Journal of Developing areas* 3 (April 1969).

16. See Clifford Wharton, ed., *Subsistence Agriculture and Economic Development* (Chicago: Aldine, 1969).

17. Richard W. van Wagenen, "Training as an Element in Bank Group Projects," *Finance and Development* (September 1972): 34-49.

18. See, for example, Arthur T. Mosher, *Creating a Progressive Rural Structure* (New York: Agricultural Development Council, 1969); Albert Waterston, "A Viable Model for Rural Development," *Finance and Development* (June 1974).

19. Donald C. Cameron, *My Tanganyika Service and Some Nigeria* (London: G. Allen and Unevin, 1939); Margery Perham, "A Restatement of Indirect Rule," *Africa* 7 (1939); Ntieyong Udo Akpan, *Epitaph to Indirect Rule* (London: Cassell, 1956).

5 LEARNING FROM IMPLEMENTATION

During the implementation stage project managers concentrate on testing design features against results in three ways, by assessing: time, to see if they are ahead or behind schedule; cost, to see if they are over or under budget; and performance, to see if goals are being met. Cultural considerations reinforce these concerns. There are four cultural criteria in project implementation: identification of critical behavioral factors; establishment of the greatest possible proximity between project events and implementors; establishment of a system of measurement to determine whether or not project goals are being achieved; and articulation of a conceptual approach toward the cultural aspects of projects that enables such lessons to be drawn as can serve as the basis for better projects in the future. If project managers or their consultants pay attention to these criteria, time, cost, and performance of implementation should benefit.

CRITICAL BEHAVIORAL FACTORS

In every project certain kinds of social change are critical to project success (for examples, see Table 5.1). By critical is meant the fact that, unless such social change takes place, the project will fail. For example, during the course of a successful nutrition project it may become obvious that the project will have minimum spread effects because new methods of food preparation will remain unpopular without increased demonstration. In an education project, the instruction may be excellent, yet all the graduates go to the cities: an indication that graduates will stay is thus a critical behavioral factor. In a resettlement project, the participants may simply walk home: an indication that permanent residence will be established is thus a critical behavioral factor.

TABLE 5.1

Behavioral Factors Affecting Implementation

Type of Project	Example of Critical Behavioral Factor	Necessary Innovations and Adaptations*
Population	Children are wanted as old-age insurance.	Smaller family size is now being accepted as economically sound.
	Population planning is considered morally wrong.	It is considered morally better to have well-cared-for family.
Education	White-collar education is considered best for children.	New enthusiasm has developed for nonformal education as a consequence of seeing that white-collar education leads to unemployment.
	Education for girls is not accepted.	Education for girls is seen to be potentially useful.
Improved livestock	Numbers of cattle owned is valued, rather than quality of livestock.	Smaller numbers of high-quality animals come to confer status similar to that accruing to those with large numbers of animals.
Nutrition	Cereal with a particular taste is used for traditional dishes.	New hybrid varieties with different taste characteristics are accepted.
Rural development	Fatalism prevails: position in life ordained.	Confidence that they can improve their own circumstances grows among participants.
Malaria eradication	The belief that malaria is unavoidable persists.	Knowledge of nature and causes of malaria, and willingness to take measures to reduce incidence of disease, increases.

*Within an estimated target population of "X," it is necessary to have changed perceptions among "Y" families within two years.

Source: Compiled by the author.

Identification

The best way to identify critical behavioral factors is to know the existing social landscape and then to assess the opportunities for new uses of traditional knowledge and values. What cultural perceptions cause people to act as they do? Which perceptions are critical? For example, poor people may, for good reason, have little confidence in government extension agents. If those attitudes remain unchanged a project may not be fully successful. Project implementors need an inventory of participant perceptions that imperil project outcome. In the field of education, negative attitudes toward educating women or toward village life may exist (for example, among young educated males)—unless these attitudes are changed, project outcome will be imperiled.

Occasionally, critical behavioral factors stand out. If growing certain kinds of crops is considered women's work, male participation in an agricultural project may be imperiled: fear of adverse social comment may be critical because it threatens those who decide to adopt innovations.

Obviously, not all behavioral factors are critical. For example, population control projects in two different culture areas felt that the route to success was through stressing small families' ability to enjoy life. In India, one of the culture areas, attitudes toward family size were strongly influenced by economic arguments, that is, the cost of having children. In South America, the other culture area, attitudes toward family planning were influenced by child care considerations: smaller families made for better child care. The Indian attitude was not critical to project success since similarity existed between local perceptions and project goals. In South America, changes in local attitudes were critical because the project would fail without them.

Selecting Critical Factors

With every successful project, social change must take place; if no social change is to take place there is probably no need for a project. These social changes must be described, ranked, and given some weight so that the most critical can be identified. For example, in a livestock project in Mali aimed at increasing livestock production of drought-stricken nomads by improving pastures through prevention of overgrazing and by improving livestock quality, the behavioral factors to be considered are the following: (1) ability to learn the new range of management techniques, (2) participants' ability to alter their perspectives that owning large numbers of poor cattle is preferable to owning small numbers of high-quality animals, and (3) willingness of nomadic peoples to adopt a sedentary way of life. The critical behavioral factor is probably (3), followed by (2), and then (1).

In a population project in South America, key obstacles to change might involve male perceptions of reproductive behavior; the contraceptive technology employed; the behavior of medical personnel to their clients; religious beliefs; perceptions of infant care, mortality and old-age needs; and educational attainments of participants. These factors must then be ranked so that the degree of change in those deemed to be critical can be assessed during the implementation process.

An agricultural population project in Turkey seeks to persuade farmers to produce new cash crops so that the supply of opium poppies can be more rigidly controlled. Obviously, there are a number of behavioral opportunities for change; however, the critical behavioral issue in this type of project concerns whether farmers can abandon production of a crop that they do not perceive to be dangerous and that is tied in with so many facets of their lives. Once behavioral factors have been assessed and the most critical identified, attention can shift to other important stages in the implementation process.

Concerns that have surfaced during the inventory of cultural resources and the design stages must be highlighted, discussed, sharpened, and acted on during the implementation process. This means that designers and implementors must ask themselves what kinds of opportunities exist and what sorts of things must change if the project is to succeed. Project design will have evaluated ways of learning, the extent of existing motivation to learn, presence of any real cultural barriers, and so on. However, changes are yet to occur, and the task of implementors is to assure occurrence of such change in those areas critical to project success.[1]

PROXIMITY

An accurate and timely flow of information during the life of a project is essential for effective management and ensuring that project redesign, where necessary, will be properly handled. Because the outcome of projects designed to reach the poorest is uncertain, it is very important to be able to effect changes as necessary. Prompt action can save a project or take advantage of overachievement. As a rule, it is best to concentrate on only the kinds of information that are essential, that is, critical behavioral factors, as opposed to information that "it would be nice to know." Close scrutiny of performance is essential: the longer the lines of communication, the greater the danger that significant events will go unobserved.

Project Implementation Organization

It is vital that an integrated project organization be established in close proximity to the participants. By integrated is meant having all specialist components—medical, social science, and agricultural—report to, and be subordinate to,

TABLE 5.2

Monitoring and Evaluation Procedures

Changes in behavior associated with a project must be shown to have taken place as a consequence of project activities. Evaluation and monitoring must make it clear that those changes would not have occurred without project intervention. This means that full information on the project area and those areas where spread effects are anticipated must be available prior to the initiation of project activities.

Impact can be measured through answering such questions as: What kinds of change have or have not taken place, and in what areas? Have changes taken place in accordance with predictions made during the design stage? Do these changes involve the kinds of people the project was designed to affect? What components of the project have been responsible for what kinds of behavior change? To structure evaluation and monitoring to answer these questions, it is best to begin by designing a suitable instrument for measuring impact. Attention can then turn to design of a suitable sampling procedure that will be necessary to supply valid data. Following this, attention can turn to estimating causality. Though a range of statistical methods may on occasion be employed, it is unlikely that multivariant or regression analysis will be useful.

Source: Compiled by the author.

the project manager. These lines of authority should last for the life of the project. The implications of such an organization should be agreed on by all departments concerned prior to project initiation.[2] The project authority should be given discretion to undertake redesign, to increase financial provisions, and to initiate project close-out, if this is earlier than planned, all without reference to higher authority. Only with proximity can the significance of data be assessed. The need during the implementation phase is not simply for data collection but also for understanding why certain kinds of data are being produced.

Evaluation and monitoring carried out by the implementing organization should both utilize the data base provided by the inventory of cultural resources and human needs. This referral process can help to verify whether the project is having an impact on the target group. When the spread effects are also revealed, this may aid in determining where future projects ought to be located.

Monitoring is usually conducted with the object of obtaining data for management use in ensuring that the project design is being adequately implemented. Evaluation is usually conducted to show that a project meets or has met certain policy, audit, or legislative criteria, or with the object of applying what is learned from the evaluation process to other projects. It is preferable to have the same data base for evaluation and monitoring; the means of information generation should be the same and the data base should be capable of serving both needs. Differences between monitoring and evaluation should relate to the time when sampling is undertaken and uses of the data. Often an immense amount of effort is expended by a group producing data for monitoring purposes, and then at a later point another group, charged with evaluation, independently produces a similar data base. Table 5.2 describes procedures for monitoring and evaluation.

PROJECT CLOSE-OUT

If behavior of participants is changing sooner than anticipated, project life should be shortened. Proximity is also necessary to establish when project close-out activities should begin. Close-out can be viewed as a progressive series of actions that terminate each stage of the project, such as design or implementation. Termination is not to be considered only when a project nears the end of its scheduled life; termination needs to be considered throughout the life of a project. If the level of project input proves to be more than adequate, it should be scaled down. If it appears that there will be too many trainees, plans should be altered. All such possibilities must be constantly reviewed (see Figure 5.1).

The later stages of project close-out should be triggered when it is determined that behavior changes introduced by the project have become institutionalized among the target number of project participants. An assessment of spread effects should then be made; if minor uncertainties exist, the project might be continued (if costs so permit) until the requisite data are obtained.

The traditional project sequence—three to five years of problem analysis, followed by project evaluation and redesign—may not be practical. Where a pilot project addresses a vital national or regional problem that continues to worsen during the life of the project, it may be necessary to make decisions about mounting similar projects before the scheduled completion date of the ongoing project. The management information system for project monitoring and evaluation should be constructed so that it can produce the necessary information at short intervals. Traditionally, projects have been supervised as they progressed and evaluated only at the end of project life. In many countries the problems of poverty cannot await such a learning sequence.

The duration of most projects, three to five years, still reflects the needs of infrastructural development projects. Construction, training, and so on can usually be accomplished within five years (although tree crops may take longer to mature). However, 10 to 15 years may be a more realistic period when behavioral change is a factor. Time is a variable: instead of maintaining rigid forecasting and keeping to rigid schedules, it may be necessary to make changes as performance is reviewed.

FIGURE 5.1

Time, Cost, and Performance for Behavioral Change

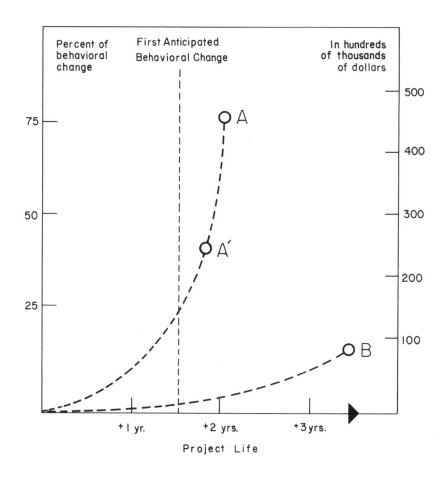

Note: A refers to data drawn from the area where the project is located; B refers to the area where spread ef fects are anticipated (see Table 6.2). At A' consideration should be given to project close-out activities. The percen of behavior change in the target population(s) is with respect to factors identified as critical (see Table 5.1).

Source: Compiled by the author.

Although an estimate of the time factor will have been made during project design, it is necessary to check continuously the progress of these (timely) behavioral changes. In an agricultural project the time required for the arrival of commodities, fertilizer, machinery, and so on will usually figure prominently in project calculations. So, too, will the point at which project output emerges in the form of trainees or crops. These considerations are often thought to be the real substance of implementation. Such reporting comments on the delivery of project assistance and the effects, in physical terms, of delivering that assistance. Infrastructural development projects concerned with bridges and dams are quite well served by this kind of treatment of time factors. It is usually the case with such projects that if men and materials are supplied, then, within a predictable period of time, results in the form of miles of road completed, participants trained, or bridges or dams built will emerge as project output.

With rural development, population, nutrition, or education projects, these traditional input-to-output calculations, while they continue to be important, must be supplemented by other considerations. A most important characteristic of such projects is that they seek to produce behavioral change: calculations about when the change must occur within the project cycle are vital. For example, how long will it take for new management and cultivational practices to become institutionalized? This kind of calculation is the most important, and the most sensitive, in the entire process of managing the behavioral dimensions of projects. It will constantly require "fine tuning," so project designs should allow for this.

MEASUREMENT

Some years ago, community development was very popular. One reason why community development lost favor was because it was not possible to measure the achievements of such an approach. Legislatures tend to distrust claims that a policy is being carried out in the absence of reliable measurement. Sooner or later there will be widespread appreciation of the fact that most of the measurements now employed, although they are useful, say too little about social change.

Neither input nor output statistics of the type now produced adequately measure social change. Nor is the length of time such changes will take measured. Records of monies disbursed, fertilizer supplied, or machinery delivered say too little about the consequences of those activities. Behavioral change, time, and associated costs must be linked (see Figure 5.1). Social change may well have not occurred even at a time when the delivery of physical input is escalating sharply. For example, despite the influx of bullion from the New World in the fifteenth and sixteenth centuries, Spain continued to decline as a European power. In the Anglo French Condominium of the New Hebrides, copra production was around

FIGURE 5.2

Impact Measurement with Four Variables

This can be used to compare project and nonproject, spread and nonspread, areas.

| | Project (P) | | | | Nonproject (P̶) | | | |
| | "a" | | "b" | | "a" | | "b" | |
	I	II	I	II	I	II	I	II
Results	A	B	C	D	E	F	G	H
Nonresults								
First and second =	100	100	100	100	100	100	100	100
	100	100	100	100	100	100	100	100

A versus ___ ample, impact of project for "a" —given roman numeral I and given "a"

B versu ___ mple, impact of project for "a" —given II and "a"

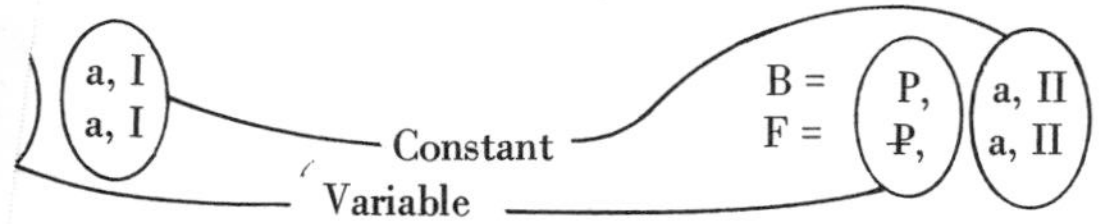

$$B = \{P, a, II\} \quad \{a, I ; a, I\}$$
$$F = \{P̶, a, II\} \quad \{a, II ; a, II\}$$

Constant

Variable

Given roman numeral and nonproject situation

To assess impac... rsus "b," hold I or II

constant and le... 'b" vary. Compare,

for example, E ...sus : E, P̶, a, I.

G, P̶, b, I.

Note: The variables are all d... (2⁴ = 16 cells), resulting in A, B, C, D, and so on, being proxies for numerals that would be percentages of column totals. Cell size will be determined b... ture project and information gathered during the inventory of cultural resources—for example, family farms, lineage, or clan groups.

Source: Compiled by the au...

79

25,000 tons in 1939; by 1960 government development expenditures had increased by well over 2,000 percent, yet copra production still stood at 25,000 tons.[3]

The reckoning of success of the "green revolution" depended largely on increases in production. In many Asian countries these increases were spectacular and it was assumed that, notwithstanding technical difficulties, the social impact was beneficial. In many instances, however, well-off farmers found it more profitable to use more fertilizer and less labor, and so the position of many poor people worsened (see Figure 5.2).

Increased Productivity, Equity, and Utilization of Benefits

Without any clear data indicating how the benefits of increased production have been distributed within a population, it may be that a project that has increased production has widened the gap between rich and poor. For example, aggregate production figures from an area where well-to-do farmers as well as poor tenant farmers may both be project participants must be disaggregated. We need to know which individuals are producing what amounts, since it might easily be the case that all production increases derive from a few prosperous individuals. For example, in a South American livestock project directed toward small holders, production increased as the number and type of project participants declined. The smallholders, under pressure from large landowners, either sold out or abandoned their new property, and the small units were absorbed in the larger and more efficient latifundia. Therefore, where increased production is envisaged as a project output, a series of samples of the poorest must be identified and monitored, with their output being compared to gross production (see Figure 5.2). Simple arithmetic will produce the sought-after comparison to the total number of project participants.

A common mistake is to measure the success of a project in terms of desired consequences. This is really a process of measuring assumptions. For example, population programs are claimed to have an impact because buildings have been constructed or so many condoms handed out. A Kenya population project that spent almost $20 million on the construction of physical facilities has had small impact on reproductive behavior. Condoms were eagerly received in one South Asian country; however, later study showed that they were being sent to urban houses of prostitution. Constructing a food processing plant or distributing food is no final indication that a project will improve the nutritional status of project participants. A livestock production project in Papua New Guinea was claimed to have beneficial consequences because it would increase the quantity of nutritious food available to poor people. What was not made clear was the fact that a pound of meat cost more than a laborer's daily wage, and there was no evidence to show that poor people would eat meat on a regular basis at such a

TABLE 5.3

Construction of Statistical Samples

Sampling strategies require close cooperation between social scientists and statisticians. The social scientist must describe all the variables that, from his point of view, may affect samples. Ordinarily, among issues to be considered are:

adequate and inadequate construction of questionnaires,
poor or efficient administration of sampling instruments,
social distance between surveyors and those interviewed,
ethnic or religious differentiation,
socioeconomic differentiation by class,
interregional or district variation,
timing of sampling, that is, frequency and duration necessary,
variability in the above issues due to different project types, and
determination of respondent settings, that is, should instruments be administered to groups or to individual men and women?

However, if the steps already recommended for the inventory of cultural resources and project design have been followed, the number of variables that must be considered will be considerably reduced. Areas with high degrees of similarity that are suitable as project areas, project spread areas, and control group areas will already be identifiable.

Questionnaire survey methods are not so useful when dealing with attitudes. In instances where it is important to gain accurate attitudinal data, it will be more useful to select a number of areas for participant observation. Social scientists should live in the areas selected for a period of at least several months.

Source: Compiled by the author.

price. The need is to measure the number of people who have benefited, to show that they are the target group identified in the inventory of cultural resources and human needs, and to show that behavior has changed and that the changed behavior will endure after the withdrawal of project assistance (see Table 5.3).

Quantitative versus Qualitative Measurement

Population projects can be measured quantitatively, in terms of lower family birthrates and, qualitatively, in terms of the socially sanctioned behavior change giving rise to that figure. Nutrition projects should not be measured in terms of food processing or storage plants erected, or amounts of food distributed. Measurement should be quantitatively and qualitatively related to behavior change in order to show the numbers of poor people utilizing and enjoying the new opportunities for better nutrition. Participation figures require accurate recording of who has participated, where these persons live, and which other individuals may reasonably be expected to participate as time passes.

It is always difficult to measure achievement in education projects qualitatively. In addition to describing the quantitative aspects (for example, numbers trained), however, one can describe individual changes. To what use has the educational experience been put? Have the roles of men and women, or those of their parents, been affected? Are educated people prepared to live in rural areas? Many people may have been trained or educated: was it the right training, the right education?

Although the nature of development projects changed substantially during the 1970s, methods of measurement have not. Input and output measurements still dominate project papers. Important as they are, such types of measurement are not enough. As Robert McNamara said at the 1970 Conference on International Economic Development held at Columbia University in New York City: "We ... require ... relevant 'development indicators' that go beyond the measure of growth in total output."

CONCEPTUAL APPROACH

Many project managers now talk of carrying out projects directed toward the poorest in an experimental mode.[4] The virtue of this is that it emphasizes the uncertain nature of project outcome and it also stresses the need to learn from projects. Using this analogy, project design can be thought of as hypothesis setting; implementation then becomes refining and restatement of the hypothesis.

Donor Performance

Innovation and adaptation concern donors as well as recipients. This is why the total project environment should be examined. It is all too frequently the case that projects never really examine the efficiency and effectiveness with which their assistance is delivered. Project papers usually justify a project and then show how it is to be carried out. Many official evaluations of projects completed after all project funds have been disbursed examine how well the participants performed. They may even mention how well a ministry or other entity given responsibility for executing the project did. But there is also a need to evaluate the work of those who originally approved the project, as well as those who supplied finance or who continued to monitor performance. All aspects that affect a project must be examined, and their respective influences weighed, if project managers are to assess correctly the reasons for under- or over-performance.

The whole system used by donors needs to be examined in terms of the principles of contextualism and incrementalism.[5] To what extent do donor requirements fit a particular country's needs? Are allowances made for the nature and availability of locally trained manpower? If the object, for donors, is gradually to work themselves out of a job, those donors must question the reality of a particular country's ever being able to operate its project system satisfactorily. It may be necessary for donors to adjust their requirements.

Increased Organizational Implementation Capacity

The second thing to consider, since an object of most project assistance is to increase the capacity of the executing organization to carry out such projects, is whether indeed that organization will be in a better position to carry out this kind of a project at the conclusion of project assistance. After all, one of the implicit notions underlying any project should be that the implementation capacity of the executing organization will be increased.

It is important continually to simplify the project process so that the project cycle can be carried out by local government units rather than central governments only. To this end, the financial requirements, personnel requirements, and operating procedures of the implementing organization should be examined to see if changes should be made. Project procedures may themselves be an obstacle to progress.[6]

Many projects are completed satisfactorily but then collapse when project assistance is withdrawn. The easiest way to guard against collapse is to design the project so that support is withdrawn before the end of the project. If performance is maintained, it can be reasonably assumed that the organization's implementation capacity has improved. The actual decision as to when to withdraw advisers is best left to the implementation stage; it is a matter of judgment based on performance.

To make such a judgment about withdrawal, those responsible for project implementation must use their knowledge of the state of the project and their proximity to events to establish and continually adjust two dates. The first is the date when project participants will be able to function without project assistance because they have institutionalized new behavior patterns. The second date is deduced by estimating when the maximum feasible number of participants will have institutionalized the new patterns. Thus, the project assistance completion date and the project goal achievement date will be different. These dates ought to be finally determined by project implementors.

Participant Performance

Should the design of this type of project be altered in the future? Were the incentives meaningful and were the intended participants able to take advantage of what was offered? Was the training or extension work as good as it should have been? Did both men and women join in? Were some people against the project? An assessment of how the participants viewed the project's impact is required.

Project managers need a bottom-up view—the view of the participants—as a check on other kinds of performance data. Most official reporters do, after all, have a vested interest in ensuring that project performance is on schedule. Participant views are very important not only during the life of the project but also during redesign, since other projects may benefit from participant suggestions. While it is important to find out why people are participating in the project, it is equally important to find out why others are not participating, particularly if their participation was originally sought by project design.[7]

Spread Effect

The final consideration involves the need to make some assessment of spread effects generated by the project. Location, type, magnitude, and time are all things that should be considered. Where are the spread effects being experienced? What kinds of things are spreading? How large is the impact and what numbers of people are involved? How long will the process take before some definite results are to be seen? Are there any obvious lessons on spread effects to be learned from this project that can be applied in future projects? This involves an assessment of the likelihood of spread or replicability. Before proceeding to examine how these needs can be met, project managers need to consider their project goals carefully.

Establishing Broad Success Indicators

Where increased production is the index of success, a project might be thought unsuccessful if it reached 60, 80, or 90 percent of the target production figure of the original design plans. An advantage of specification of different implementation assessments is that it enables project managers to estimate success and failure of their projects in more realistic and accurate terms than is the case when success is measured solely in terms of levels of production, levels of income for project participants, or construction of buildings or miles of road.

Using the four assessments proposed above, and bearing in mind the need to learn from projects, it can be seen that a project might fail to meet design estimates of performance for participant involvement and yet be successful. For example, a project may fail to meet increased production estimates, but achieve substantial spread effects. Another project may fail to achieve either spread effects or increased production targets, but substantially increase the implementation capacity of the organization executing the project. Projects that have been defined as successful because during the life of the project they achieved certain levels of production may, in fact, have minimal behavioral consequences. Increases in production, even when attributable to the project, may decline when advisers leave: the results may have been obtained at a much higher cost than necessary, the participants may not have acquired any new knowledge or skills, or spread effects may not have developed.

RECOGNIZING SOCIAL CHANGE IN IMPLEMENTATION

Projects whose success depends primarily on achieving social change are more difficult to implement than projects where social change is subsidiary to a primary goal of construction. Infrastructural projects involving engineering and construction are examples of the latter type. The designers of such projects can form predictions with some confidence and thus be fairly certain about the outcome of construction efforts within a given period of time. With infrastructural projects, the implementation phase can be distinguished from the planning phase. In such projects implementation is somewhat mechanical—it can often be monitored from site records, engineers' reports, and so on. Problems are likely to involve the nonarrival of commodities, a delay occasioned by bad weather, labor disputes, faulty engineering work, and so on: the range of problems may be fairly narrow and predictable. The social change elements in the projects, although they do, of course, ultimately affect people, are secondary and often assumed rather than explicitly treated by project papers. Obviously, construction projects do have severe problems on occasion; however, the state of the art is fairly advanced—there is a body of knowledge, a reservoir of successful experiences about how to do things. In addition, those who actually engage in construction and so on have done it many times before: apart from problems of training, most of the problems they encounter are of a physical nature.

The nature of implementation in rural development, education, nutrition, population, and health projects where social change is a primary goal, is a different matter—and even more so with projects directed toward the poorest. In these projects it is not usually possible to draw a neat line between the design and implementation phases: design may intrude upon implementation and implementation must constantly be considered (see Table 5.4). In fact, implementation begins during the design stage. There are a number of reasons why this is so, among then the fact that it is difficult to calculate the reaction of project participants to future events and stimuli. The ways in which a road can efficiently be built

TABLE 5.4

Summary of Cultural Appraisal System*

Project Cycle Process		Criteria	Forward and Backward Linkages
Identifying poorest (Chapter 3)	1	Identification of groups	5,6,10,14,15
	2	Social organization	1,3,7,8,11,15,16,18,19
	3	Belief systems	1,2,4,6,7,11,15,17
	4	Wealth forms	1,2,3,6,11,13,15,17,20
	5	Patterns of mobility	1,2,10,14,15,17
	6	Analytical description of poorest	1-20
Designing projects (Chapter 4)	7	Contextualism	1-6,13,14,15,16
	8	Incrementalism	2,10,11,12,13,15,16
	9	Minimum participant profile	6,7,8,10
	10	Spread effects	1,2,7,8
	11	Motivation	1-6,13,17
	12	Time factors	1-6,11,17,19
	13	Benefit incidence	1,2,11,14,17
	14	Communication	1-3,5,9,15,16
	15	Design of extension efforts	1,2,5,10,16,17,18
	16	Using indigenous organization	1,2,3,7,14,17,18
Learning from implementation (Chapter 5)	17	Critical behavioral factors	1,2,3,9
	18	Proximity	1,2,5,12,15,16
	19	Project close-out	10,12,17

*The criteria advanced for the appraisal of projects form a system, thus change in one of the criteria inevitably affects other criteria. Since the criteria are logically interconnected it is important to appreciate the forward and backward linkages that emphasize the unity of the system.

Source: Compiled by the author.

are known to a degree, but knowledge about how one produces behavioral change is much less certain.

Of course, it would be preferable to make the social change goals of infrastructural projects primary. Certainly a good number of road projects would have been more successful had they been thought of as experiments in social change rather than construction projects. Every project involving construction or other infrastructural components has an impact on people. New opportunities for travel or work, which ultimately affect behavior, will be created. What presently distinguishes the infrastructural project is that success, which should be measured in behavioral terms, tends to be measured in physical terms. Tokyo's new international airport should have been viewed in terms of its social dimensions rather than as a construction project: as a construction project it might be considered successful, as a socially relevant project, disastrous. Success should also be measured in terms of social change, seeking to know what people have done with opportunities created as a consequence of project construction.

NOTES

1. There are a number of important publications, among them: Development Alternatives, Inc., "Strategies for Small Farmer Development," a report prepared for AID (Washington, D.C.: Development Alternatives, May 1975); Uma Lele, *The Design of Rural Development* (Baltimore: Johns Hopkins University Press, 1975); Albert Waterston, "A Viable Model for Rural Development," *Finance and Development* 11, no. 2 (June 1974).

2. See, for example, S. N. Eisenstadt, "Institutionalization and Change," *American Sociological Review* 29 (1964): 235-47; Hiram S. Philips, *Guide for Development: Institution Building and Reform* (New York: Praeger, 1969).

3. James S. G. Wilson, *Economic Survey of the New Hebrides* (London: Her Majesty's Stationery Office, 1965). Wilson supposed that development could take place if Melanesians were taxed into working on plantations. Once faced with materialism, he supposed that they would acquire a new pattern of preferences. It was the kind of thinking that needs to be done, even if the conclusions were a bit wild. See the author's review in *Economica*, New Series, 35, no. 138 (May 1968).

4. Lele, *The Design of Rural Development*, p. 130; Robert Chambers and Deryck Belshaw, *Managing Rural Development*, discussion paper no. 15 (Brighton, England: Institute for Development Studies, 1973).

5. Donald C. Stove, "Removing Administrative and Planning Constraints to Development," *Journal of Administration Overseas* 12, no. 1 (January 1973); Chi-Yuen We, "Training in Public Administration for Development," *Journal of Administration Overseas*, no. 1 (January 1971). Guy Hunter has recently pointed up this eclipse of noneconomic social science skills in "The Implementation of Agricultural Development: Towards Criteria for the Choice of Tools," *Agricultural Administration* 1, no. 1 (1974): 51-72.

6. Dennis A. Rondinelli, "International Requirements for Project Preparation: Aids or Obstacles to Development Planning," *Journal of American Institute of Planners* 42, no. 3 (July 1976). He makes the valuable point that project procedures must adapt to local capacity rather than the sophisticated standards that prevail in industrial countries. See also Edgar Owens, "The Local Development Program of East Pakistan," *International Development Review* 9 (March 1967).

7. See, for example, *The Social and Economic Implications of Large-Scale Introduction of New Varieties of Food Grain* (Geneva: UN Research Institute for Social Development, 1974); Anthony Leeds, "The Significant Variables Determining the Character of Squatter Settlements," *America Latina* 12, no. 3 (1969); Ernest Schumacher, *Small Is Beautiful: Economics as if People Mattered* (New York: Harper & Row, 1974).

6 DATA REQUIREMENTS FOR CULTURAL APPRAISAL

Project managers who have to handle the cultural appraisal of projects usually have two questions, both equally important: how do you get the data you need and how do you know when you have the right data? As with project design, the simpler the data collection, the better. High-powered team research and sophisticated mathematical analysis, perhaps using computers, will usually be out of place. Data collection systems should, as far as possible, be contextual and incremental.

The guidance given in this chapter is not intended as a comprehensive blueprint, a teaching "how-to-do-it." For the project manager with sufficient social science background, this chapter should serve as an aide-mémoire. For the project manager with little social science background, this chapter should reinforce a disposition to obtain suitable social science assistance. If a project manager needs thorough instructions, external assistance is undoubtedly required. In such cases the chapter can illustrate the general advantages of various kinds of data so that project managers can enter into a useful dialogue with social scientists. Social scientists may find the analysis of project types a useful aide-mémoire. The data is based on personal experience in various countries and an in-depth analysis of World Bank projects.

Previous chapters have identified principal data requirements for mapping cultural resources and for project design and implementation. Existing data must be matched against the requirements before decisions on design revision are taken. Quality of quantitative data roughly correlates with a particular country's level of socioeconomic development: very poor countries have very poorly developed data collection systems, and what is collected is usually not very accurate. In such countries, accurate quantitative data concerning attitudes, values and beliefs, or production output (acreage, mileage, and so on) are usually unavailable.

Assessments of what people want or feel may be based on supposition. Often figures on new trees planted or new lands cleared or placed under cultivation are produced by people who have no idea of what an acre or hectare actually is—kilos and tons of production may be counted by people who have only a vague idea of what a kilo or a ton actually is. In parts of West Africa, for example, weight is equated with lorry load.

There are a number of reasons why yields are hard to estimate from farmers' own records and data: harvesting may be spread over some months so that totals are neither noticed nor recorded; harvesting may fail to record the amount used for family consumption and for barter, recording only cash sales in local markets; figures may be deliberately falsified to avoid taxes or rent increases by landlords; and markets may be officially controlled, resulting in extensive smuggling and black-market trading.

Crop-cutting surveys are one method of getting more accurate data. A sample area of land is harvested under supervision. From this sample yields can be calculated with some accuracy. However, to be valid this method needs crops that are customarily harvested at one time and well-cleared, open lands of uniform fertility. Crops produced in tropical rain forests or in rough, broken country are not suited to the crop-cutting technique. In some instances, the number of economic trees and the number and weight of bunches of fruit must be counted comprehensively. Samples can only be constructed when there is assurance that data are representative. A satisfactory method, assuming that plots and families have been linked, is to assess yields prior to harvesting. Cocoa, coconuts, coffee, and so on can be estimated by an experienced agriculturalist, as can grain crops, tubers, and various legumes.

Project managers should guard against bias in reporting. Figures may be inflated to please or impress: figures may be reduced to avoid scrutiny, jealousy, or even higher taxes. Productivity might even be inflated by biased data collectors who are seeking an indication of ethnic superiority and leadership in the struggle to modernize. When asked to collect data on the attitudes and aspirations of very poor people, collectors often produce the kinds of data they know their superiors want to see; thus, data collection often confirms planners' ideas of what poor people really want. It is important to ensure that alternative or contrary ideas—to those suggested by a particular project— have a chance to appear. Data should be able to deny as well as confirm.[1]

QUESTIONNAIRE SURVEYS

With quantitative data, project managers must be able to feel confident that the figures are valid and reliable. Household surveys and other kinds of questionnaires are often required for project design calculations.[2] These surveys seek figures on production, distribution, consumption, attitudes, values, beliefs, income, aspirations, and so on. Project managers can question themselves and those responsible for the collection and dissemination as to which quantitative data will reveal the important strengths and weaknesses of project implementation.

General Characteristics

The strength of well-designed questionnaire surveys lies in their ability to answer specific questions that project managers may have, and to answer these authoritatively by means of sampling. A further advantage is usually thought to lie in the fact that administration of questionnaire surveys can be carried out by low-level manpower. The methods and techniques associated with questionnaire surveys are also better known and more readily accepted by most project managers than are qualitative data.

The weaknesses involved with questionnaire surveys spring from their often having been designed by people with no real understanding of the social circumstances of those who are surveyed. One must know what kinds of questions are permissible. Can one properly ask what kind of education a man wants for his children, or whether he and his wife want to have children? Is it permissible to ask about incomes? Will people fear that giving honest answers will cause their taxes to increase or that they may have broken some law? People may be ashamed of their position in life and may not want to have their distress recorded. It is a matter for wonderment that people who would not, in their home communities, address a stranger unless introduced—and whose deeper feelings are seldom revealed to their wives and closest friends—should habitually assume that questionnaire surveys will, in some miraculous way, evoke a completely different response in others.

Design Considerations

Expert advice is needed to determine what kinds of questions can be asked and also how such questions should be phrased.[3] Questions must take language differences into account, as well as values, beliefs, and attitudes. Expert advice is also needed to determine who should be asked which questions: whoever designs questionnaires should know about socioeconomic status and about differences between groups, occupations, and sexes. Finally, expert advice is required to determine who should administer the questionnaires. Will the best results be obtained by training people drawn from similar communities to administer questionnaires? What level of education, what status, what ethnicity, or what sex should those administering the surveys have? How long must survey staff spend in a village before administering questionnaires? These considerations are espe-

TABLE 6.1

Construction of Questionnaires

A small amount of high-quality data is preferable to a large amount of error-ridden data. Questionnaire construction is a "chicken-and-egg" problem because a certain amount of information must already be available. Consideration of the following factors is recommended.

Presurvey Resources

Qualifications and experience of those who will construct questionnaire: An anthropologist or sociologist at M.A. level familiar with the language and customs of those to be studied is essential.

Training for those who will administer questionnaire: What age and educational level should those administering the questionnaires possess? How many administrators are needed? Should men work with women respondents, or vice versa?

Implications of project characteristics: How long a period should questioning cover and when should questioning take place; for example, is harvesting piecemeal or seriatim? Must one wait five to seven years till tree crops mature? Is there a known calendar of important ritual events spread over so many months?

Motivation of respondents: It is useful to require administrators of questionnaires to assess why it is that respondents answer questions? What do respondents think the data is for?

Length and content: One way to assess whether designers of questionnaires are sensitive to matter of length and content is to ask what would be too long and what kinds of questions cannot be asked.

Sample design: Statistical analysis will be useful in handling sampling errors, precision, reliability, and so on.

Instead of relying on one presurvey and then launching into full-scale administration, it may be better to gradually perfect the instrument and the method of administration. It may be necessary to vary methods for different regions or sexes. Administration of the questionnaires should consider the following factors.

Format of questions: Because those who administer questionnaires will inevitably be associated with officialdom, questions asking farmers to say what they learned, or did not learn, from extension agents are unwise. It is better to say "some farmers think this, some think that, what do you think?"

Context: Sometimes administration to a group will be more accurate than individual administration. Sometimes short lists will be preferable to long lists. Sometimes it will be better to ask the questions and record the answers later rather than asking respondents to reply privately.

Source: Compiled by the author.

cially important where data are to be collected in communities with low literacy levels and little history of having received benefits from officials (see Table 6.1).

There are advantages and disadvantages of various staffing options. Well-educated survey workers may be reluctant to spend adequate amounts of time in "backward" villages and may wish to emphasize social distance between themselves and the village. If local people are trained as survey workers and they turn out to be unsatisfactory, then it may be hard to dismiss them because they may then have adverse effects on the project. The best survey workers are unrelated to those in the survey village, possess appropriate language skills, and have career prospects.

Past Events

In assessing data, project managers must decide whether data have been collected with sufficient frequency and if there have been adequate time intervals between collection. Can one usefully ask farmers about agricultural input used two or three years ago? Data on social conditions are frequently out-of-date. For example, many anthropological and sociological accounts are 10 or 15 years old. If rapid social change is taking place, this is a dangerous situation for validity and reliability.

Frequency and periodicity must be explicitly considered for agricultural production in most projects where social change is vital. Very often farmers remember only significant events, such as a very lean year or a very good year, and questions about seeds used, labor input, and manure or fertilizer may not be useful because such things are not considered worth remembering. It may be necessary to collect data as farming operations take place instead of waiting till the next growing season. A conscientious decision about reporting periods should be taken, based on actual, on-the-ground investigations.

In most rural communities, the time when an event being investigated can be established by referring to particularly significant past happenings—World War II, an earthquake, when a bridge was built, when a particular government official was in charge of a district. In the Solomon Islands, examples of such events were the landing of the U.S. Marines on Guadalcanal in 1942, the murder of a well-known district officer in 1928, and so on. A schedule of such events can be drawn up for most areas.

If is often necessary to try to understand the age structure of a population in the absence of reliable demographic data. There are simple physical tests for age, such as the loss of milk teeth, the onset of menstruation (12-14 years) for girls, and the growth of underarm hair for boys (14-16 years). Where more sophisticated calibration is required, tests can often be obtained from police (who need such data for criminal cases) or physicians.

Sampling

Project managers concerned with population or nutrition projects should pay attention to ensuring that their data cover valid and reliable samples. Population samples, when broken down by age, sex, and class, have often been too small to establish statistical significance. Regardless of whether samples are of individuals, families, lineages, tribes, or villages, one must be aware of the social landscape before determining sampling units: what is a typical individual, a typical family, or a typical village? Samples must be based on an understanding of the representativeness of the data to be employed. Social mapping, if it has been properly carried out, can be very helpful here.

Samples must also be constructed in such a way that surveys can be carried out speedily, as required for management decisions. If few survey researchers are available, the sample may have to be small; where large numbers are available, it may be possible to survey an entire village. Surveys based on questionnaire administration should not last more than a month. If surveys take longer, memories may lapse and respondents may have inaccurate preconceptions about the purposes and meaning of the survey.[4]

Samples must be comprehensive if at all possible. The population from which samples are drawn covers the entire area where project effects are anticipated. A common mistake is to survey the participants while failing to survey project staff or cooperating officials. Samples should cover the project environment and meet the criteria advanced in the chapter on implementation. Care must also be exercised to ensure that samples deal with a broader social scene than villages and households alone.

Village information built up of household data may obscure significant factors affecting the acceptance or rejection of innovation. For example, men on the Micronesian island of Yap wanted as many children as possible, yet their wives privately disagreed and habitually aborted themselves: the principles underlying reproductive behavior on Yap might not be discovered through household samples. Where power is exercised by religious leaders or by male secret societies, household samples will also have limited utility. Data should cover the criteria given in the chapters on cultural resources, mapping, and project design.

PARTICIPANT OBSERVATION

Project managers seeking to assess the validity and reliability of data on attitudes, values, and beliefs will encounter the anthropological methods and techniques known as "participant observation." This refers to the means most anthropologists have used to collect their data since Bronislaw Malinowski's pioneering work in the Trobriand Islands of the Western Pacific in the years following World War I. Anthropological field work begins with a sustained period of immersion in the culture. The anthropologist "joins" the community for a period of one to two years, learning the language, living as a member of the community, and recording data as a participant observer. Familiarity with language, seasonal activities, and the entire round of community affairs allows the anthropologist to get close to events.[5]

Method

The anthropological field worker relies on a number of informants to supply data. Ideally, information from one informant can be checked against that of another. Anthropologists usually try to use a number of informants of different sex, socioeconomic status, age, and so on. The informants should be representative of the social milieu; their number should permit adequate cross-checking of the data.

The one to two years allowed for field work is the usual time period associated with a first visit. The first visit is usually associated with pursuit of a doctoral dissertation. Subsequent visits to a field work area should not require more than a few months. The length of the initial visit is not merely occasioned by the fact that the first visit is a training visit for the anthropologist; it is also necessary that the entire environment be surveyed before decisions on appropriate research strategies for specialized issues are made.

Strengths and Weaknesses

The strength of this method of data collection is that it can produce data of high quality. It becomes possible for the anthropological investigator to understand why certain kinds of data are produced: he or she can understand why production figures are high or low, why people want more land, or why health facilities are used or unused. A further strength in this kind of data collection is the fact that any anthropologist exposed to this initial field experience inevitably develops a reservoir of experience that is not apparent in publications. Questions can be asked of such an anthropologist long after he or she has left the field. In this way the full value of the field work can be garnered.[6]

Some weaknesses of field work are that it is carried out individually and that it is hard to draw results of wide-ranging geographical significance from such studies. An individual anthropologist, if male, may have trouble collecting material on female aspects of childbirth. A female anthropologist may have similar problems assessing male attitudes. Anthropologists choose particular locations because the social conditions are unique: it therefore becomes important to ask what general considerations can be extrapolated from such studies.

ADEQUACY OF THE DATA BASE

The data base, a mixture of quantitative and qualitative elements, must be such that it permits constant monitoring of project participant behavior in the light of the criteria advanced in previous chapters. Does the government have good sources of information on the people where the project is located? How are data collected and analyzed? When single-source informational resources are being assessed, covering, for example, farmers' attitudes, women's aspirations, or the socioeconomic position of adopters of new innovations, two tests can be employed.

The first test is an assessment of authenticity. Where data are produced from a single source, as with official statistics, is any independent verification, or means of verification, of the data provided? Are the data accurate and representative?

Where independent verification of single-source data cannot be carried out, project managers should themselves attempt to achieve such verification if the integrity of the data is vital to project success. Quantitative data derived from questionnaire surveys should always be checked very carefully to ensure that there is no distortion. The methodology employed in questionnaire surveys, personnel used, representativeness of the sample, and manner in which investigators are regarded by the people living in the sample area should always be indicated.

The second test of single-source data assesses objectivity. Where official information is collected and disseminated, one must assess the motivation underlying the donation of data. Why do respondents answer personal questions? Why are certain kinds of data collected and disseminated? Information can be relied on only when underlying motivation has been established. Project participants and officials may have a number of reasons for giving information, such as fear, pride, hope of promotion, or patriotism. People do not usually provide information simply because they believe in well-designed projects.

COLLECTION OF DATA

Project managers should personally check quantitative and qualitative data on the ground level. In addition to assessing the accuracy and reliability of data, they can use these observations toward development of adequate data collection procedures. The kinds of data that need to be checked on the ground level include, as previously mentioned, production, income, calorie intake, births, deaths, acreages, and so on (see Table 6.2). The data must make clear the project situation and must include not only information on the project location but also on areas where spread effects are anticipated.

Table 6.2

Required Quantitative Baseline Measures

Evaluation of the Preproject Situation

Characteristics of the situation, such as a reproductive rate of 35 per 1,000, caloric intake of 2,000 per day, literacy rate of 2 percent, the monetary income of poorest, and the presence or absence of particular skills and knowledge, are important.

Definition of Samples

Three (six, if possible) groups should, at minimum, be identified:

A. In the area to receive project input,
B. In the area ultimately to be affected by spread effects,
C. In an area similar to A but where no project impact is anticipated.

Choice of Samples

Sample groups should be as nearly identical as possible in respect to, for example, size, social structure and organization, values and beliefs, resources, and language and environment.

Schematic of Samples

Samples can be represented graphically as follows:

B   A   C

Monitoring and Evaluation

Time, cost, and performance should be monitored and evaluated in A, B, and C:

By comparing A with B and C, results attributable to the project can be estimated.
By comparing B with A and C, results attributable to spread effects can be estimated.
By comparing C with A and B, results attributable to the project can be estimated.

Source: Compiled by the author.

Identification of Groups

The best way to uncover differences among groups that are significant enough for recording is to visit widely, interacting with the widest possible range of people. The problem does not lend itself to questionnaire survey methods; rather, participant observation by one or more persons (depending on country size) is preferred. Three sets of questions will uncover most differences. One seeks information about different ethnic groups and how they usually interact. Is there tension, fighting, or cooperation? A second refers to "modernization" and the progress of various groups or geographical regions. Which groups are thought to be advanced, which backward?

In many nations where tensions between ethnic groups are high, discussion of ethnic differences is strongly discouraged. National unity and the need to project a national consensus discourage attempts to identify ethnic separateness. Another objection sometimes raised against social mapping is that mapping can be thought colonialist in ideology. Those who make this charge suspect mappers of wishing to preserve archaic social distinctions whereas they, the critics, seek extraordinary or revolutionary social change.[7]

An answer to these objections is that there is no necessary evil in social mapping; rather, it is an attempt to produce better projects in order to avoid wasting resources. It can be shown that in most countries where strong inter-group antagonisms exist failure to allow for such situations in project planning leads to poor results. Social mapping is not judgmental—it merely seeks to describe the existing situation as it is.

In North Malaita, in the Solomon Islands, differentiation exists between social groups that live in the inland hills and worship their ancestors and those that live within easy reach of the sea, which are Christian. Ethnic cleavages are not so strong. The Christian group views itself as progressive, literate, money-making, and healthy. The ancestor worship group views itself as backward, unhealthy, and malnourished. Members of the two groups do not cooperate and are either hostile toward each other or, at best, indifferent. The distinction between the groups is based on geography, since the coastal people had greater access to government and missionary personnel. The inland people had no way to earn money because copra and cocoa were not suited to their environment. The same kind of distinction can be seen between plains people and hill people in Burma and other Southeast Asian countries, such as Thailand, Laos, and Cambodia.

The third series of questions about social classes was not important in Malaita, although elucidation of class differences may be very important in other countries. For example, in Peru there are several well-defined social classes: at the top are the descendants of Spanish colonists; at the bottom of the social pyramid are the aboriginal Indian inhabitants, or Cholos. In India, there were traditionally four well-defined classes: priests, warriors, merchants, and untouchables. Although the passage of time has lessened the impact of some of these divisions in Indian society, some of them must still be taken into account.[8]

The best way to test whether intergroup differences have been discovered is to make sure that some are identified in the course of a survey. No country is without some such distinctions, whether among ethnic groups, between the supposed advanced and the backward, or between those of high social status and those of low status. This process, if undertaken on a full-time basis, should not take more than two man-months.

Social Organization

It is almost impossible to appreciate the nature of land tenure arrangements in a country solely by reading books written by anthropologists or legislation on land tenure. Anthropological coverage is seldom complete and may cover only a small number of traditional areas. Land tenure legislation is usually directed toward primogeniture and thus may not affect wide areas held under traditional tenure.

Within the chosen sample, the land belonging to or being used by each household or family should be mapped out. That is, a plan of the village should numerically identify each household. Each household should be associated with its lands in nearby farming areas, the size of the plot or plots being carefully measured. Often boundaries are hard to identify, particularly in broken country or wooded areas. It is often the case that families may have different parcels of land—one used for grazing, another for gardens, and another for producing timber and other materials used in house construction (see Table 6.3).

In areas where population fluctuates due to seasonal employment, urban migration, or dramatic increases in population growth, it is essential that data on landholdings be checked, since official records may be misleading. This can help establish whether plots are becoming smaller in response to population increase or because certain socioeconomic groups are increasing their landholdings at the expense of others.

Local court records are the most satisfactory way to obtain land tenure data. Recent cases provide a commentary on social change because they illustrate both pressures for new kinds of land tenure and those for maintenance of traditional arrangements.[9] Sufficient case data must be collected to permit a map, detailing tenure arrangements and their distribution, to be made. Court data can usually be supplemented by data from the local lands and survey department, which will have all recent surveys on record. Records should show which pieces of ground have been registered in the names of individual owners, which registration requests are pending, and which areas have the lowest number of requests.[10] Collection of such data can be accomplished within two six-man months, depending on the size and social complexity of the country involved.

To obtain data on types of family structure and work organization, investigation might begin with what happens at markets. Sensitively designed ques-

TABLE 6.3

Investigation of Land Tenure Patterns

What Is Held?

It is essential that the nature of all available types of interest in land be delineated. Ownership is a bundle of rights. These rights should be specified. In many societies, there is nothing akin to the concept of landownership found in industrial countries. For example, the owners of topsoil may be different persons than the owners of subsoil. Perhaps neither subsoil nor topsoil owners own trees that stand on their ground. These categories of rights, or what is held, must be investigated. There may be few rights that resemble ownership; instead, land-use rights may only be usufructuary. However, even in those countries where substantial areas are held under traditional tenure, it will usually be the case that large areas are also held by primogeniture, that is, the common pattern for industrial countries.

How Is It Held?

For all categories of interest in land, some performance is required on the part of the holders of those interests. For those with ownership rights, land may have to be used productively or it will be confiscated. Those with lesser interests may have to pay rent, perform ritual or economic services for kinsmen, or follow the customs of their ancestors.

Who Holds It?

In any country there will be substantial areas held or used by individuals. Other areas will be held by groups of people. The nature of the qualifications for membership in such groups must be explored. It is equally important to describe the circumstances of those who have no land-use rights.

Source: Compiled by the author.

tionnaire surveys can be used to elucidate how goods are produced and how the proceeds of sales are distributed. This will reveal patri- or matrilineal features. Questioning in villages should be directed toward the manner in which capital assets have been created. How are houses, roads, wharves, churches, clinics, schools, and so on constructed? These kinds of structures are beyond the construction capability of one household. By asking such questions it should be possible to uncover the existing forms of work organization—what their membership criteria are, how often they meet, and what constitutes the permissible range of functions under their charter. The investigations should be completed within two man-months.

Belief Systems

Both questionnaire survey and participant observation techniques should be used in studying belief systems. Samples should again be made up from the groups that social mapping has shown to be significant. Establishing the geography of religions can be a complex business: census data may be available, and missionaries can often fill in the gaps. Further useful data can sometimes be gleaned from police records, since there may be records of complaints against those who break religious injunctions. A useful way to highlight differences between belief systems is to examine the role of women.

Attitudes toward social change can be uncovered by using questionnaire survey methods to assess which cultural features respondents feel should be changed and which preserved. However, personal questioning is usually better than administration of questionnaires where population issues are involved. The first thing to be determined is how decisions about having children are made. Such questioning should be directed separately toward men and women drawn from different social groups and socioeconomic levels.

One obvious way to determine attitudes toward health is to consult medical personnel in hospitals and at dressing or first-aid stations. Both male and female personnel should be consulted. The demand for medicines and services is an important indication of attitudes. What kinds of illness are brought in for treatment? This kind of information can be supplemented by interview material drawn from sample villages. Questions should be directed toward older women and men and indigenous healers. They can be asked to list the most dangerous illnesses and appropriate kinds of cure or treatment.

Beliefs about distribution of goods and services are important to investigate. A careful record should be kept of amounts and types of food retained from yields and used for family consumption or reserve. This record should include livestock as well as grains, tubers, fruits, and other vegetables and tree crops. In addition, it is useful to record the most common methods of food preparation and actual food distribution within the family. What criteria are used for intrafamily food distribution? Do males get more than females? Do portions increase with age and seniority or with physical size?

Within the community itself, food given in exchange for goods and services enjoyed by the family should also be recorded. How much goes to the landlord or other families for satisfaction of debts contracted with stores and so on?

The portion of family production offered for sale should be recorded. Sometimes farmers are forced to sell all their marketable surplus when prices are low, sometimes they have poor leverage and must sell individually to well-organized middlemen, and sometimes they sell only when cash is required.

Productivity may be thought to be affected by failure to perform an important ritual, such as giving a feast for dead ancestors. Productivity might also be affected by exposing lands to impurity: a menstruating woman is thought responsible for infertility in certain parts of the world. Does land have to be blessed? Do important and costly rituals have to be carried out to ensure fertility?

If undertaken at the same time as other basic data gathering, collection of this type of data should require two man-months.

Wealth Forms

Wealth is a difficult topic to investigate in poor rural communities. Questionnaire surveys tend to produce inaccurate data because people are unwilling to give a precise reckoning of their wealth lest they be assessed extra taxes. Additionally, many surveys concentrate only on monetary holdings, thus ignoring important categories of indigenous wealth. However, it should be possible to cover this topic in one man-month.

Among the poorest people in any developing community, money may not be the general medium of exchange. The first task is to find out what forms of wealth exist and which kinds of social transaction those wealth forms are used for during a year. Most of this information can be obtained from studies of market transactions, analysis of household possessions, and discussion with such people as bankers and anthropologists or other social scientists working in the area. Samples should again be drawn from all groups found to be significant.

Family income may arise from a variety of sources: sale of produce, sale of labor of family members, rental of lands or equipment, sale of livestock or artifacts, remittance from urban relatives, pensions, and so on. Care must be taken to compile a representative sample and to monitor data accuracy, since people in most poor rural communities are reluctant to discuss monetary income.

Farmers' reasons for wanting a monetary income should be recorded. Is money wanted for consumer items, such as soap, salt, clothing, kerosene, bicycles, radios, and mosquito netting? Is money required to pay rents or government taxes of various kinds? Are large amounts of money required for security or as an index of status? Is money in the form of coins or specie preferred, or paper (many traditional communities dislike paper money because it quickly deteriorates)? (See also Table 3.2.)

Mobility Patterns

This data can be collected in about two man-months. Well-constructed questionnaire surveys taken at markets can establish significant patterns of movement. In most rural communities these patterns are affected by the need to reach markets, stores, medical services, police, churches, and workplaces. Participant observation inquiries directed toward medical personnel and police officials can help establish patterns of seasonal movement.[11] Medical personnel often have valuable data on the spread and containment of diseases based on mobility patterns, while police officials often have to know where to find people at particular times in a year. Local government officials also tend to know a great deal about mobility patterns. Tax officials can be a useful source for this kind of data, since they study the movements of those who pay taxes—and those who do not; agricultural, medical, or educational extension workers, on the other hand, are often not affected by the presence or absence of particular individuals in villages when they visit. They tend to see their jobs as involving visits to villages rather than contact with people.

Basic Human Needs

The matter of which categories of poor in what areas can realistically be helped is a political decision. However, that decision-making process can be helped by a supply of good, accurate data on the poor and their problems. Understanding of basic human needs is an outcome of a national inventory of cultural resources. This process cannot be satisfactorily avoided or circumvented. If national figures—income, caloric intakes, and so on—are relied on, it is unlikely that they will be either comprehensive, since narrow samples are often biased, or accurate, since a tendency to aggregate and average data dominates such exercises. Useful data can be collected within one man-month.

REVIEWING PROJECT DESIGN

Previous chapters have concentrated on project managers who must identiiy, design, and implement projects while handling the cultural dimensions themselves or obtaining assistance from social scientists. There are, however, many occasions when project managers inherit projects identified and designed by others. Guidance is given below on the kinds of behavioral problems typically encountered with some common project types. This treatment focuses on issues that should, as much as possible, be viewed along lines suggested in previous chapters.

INTRODUCTION OF NEW CROP TYPES

Frequently, projects to introduce new types of crops pay insufficient attention to existing forms of social organization. The issues treated in the chapter on project design, Chapter 4, need emphasis. The cultivation of certain types of crops entails a cycle of activities that have social, and possibly ritual, significance.

Change may affect the utilization pattern of land and labor. Distribution of time calculations by potential project participants will be important.

A first step is to examine the incentives from the individual's, and then from the association's, point of view in order to assess motivation. Are changes in the design of the project called for? Shifts in the distribution of power, wealth, and status and their effects on the group can be assessed along lines suggested when benefit incidence was discussed with respect to project design. Are long-term structural realignments within the group called for? Are credit arrangements satisfactory? What will the consequences of the new income generation be on purchasing power and leisure time? Will migration to cities be affected? Will crop specialization have any marked effect on nutrition and reproductive behavior?

Estimation of spread effects is particularly important. If macrolevel data are available, experienced consultants should be able to collect these kinds of data in two weeks. What is the relationship between this project and the wider society? Is the project special to this region or group of people? Are the results capable of emulation and are the necessary measures an explicit part of the project design? What kinds of evidence suggest that the project will be enthusiastically supported? What is the attitude of local leaders and opinion makers? What decisions are asked of participants? Can the positive and negative features of these decisions be elucidated? Given a basic concern with subsistence needs, does the project alter the basic confidence of the participant in his or her ability to provide for a family? If success seems to depend largely on the quality of government or other official intervention, what is the local opinion of officialdom?

RESETTLEMENT PROJECTS

A starting point in seeking critical behavioral factors is the pattern of recruitment: reasons for participating in projects and the kinds of satisfaction offered. The dissatisfied can often simply walk home.[12] This action in itself is a critical behavioral problem. Disgruntled people who have not been notably successful in one community do not always have the potential for success in another. The best form of recruitment involves the total community—the removal of a viable community from one area to another. No matter what the method of recruitment, one must know what the settlers have been told they will obtain. Random selection of settlers is problematic when the people come from different ethnic groups and communities. It may be difficult to achieve a viable settler community. Will the resettlement be viewed as a lowering or raising of status? To what extent has the group been consulted before resettlement? Data on motivation can usually be collected within two weeks.

The next factor is the envisaged pattern of organization for the new community. Is there a departure from traditional forms and, if so, is there reason to believe that it will be unattainable? Here it is necessary not only to envisage patterns of organization in the economic sphere but also the political, the social, and the religious forms of organization common to the settlers. What is the relationship envisaged between the new community and neighboring communities? Will the neighboring communities view the scheme, for instance, as an attempt to preempt their uncultivated (but cultivable) lands?

As already indicated, design of such projects must pay special attention to contextual and incremental factors. New settlements appear to present opportunities to devise new systems of tenure capable of overcoming what are thought to be inappropriate features of traditional systems. But there is a need to appreciate that a tenure system is a reflection of a social system, not a capricious or arbitrary feature, the alteration of which will automatically be greeted with relief by settlers. What are the functions of the traditional system; to what extent are these made redundant by resettlement? How was the area of resettlement obtained, and from whom?

What is the nature of the residence pattern proposed under the resettlement scheme? Are the proposed patterns different from existing patterns; do they, for instance, envisage nuclear family residence as opposed to joint family residence? Does the new pattern alter family relationships and authority? Is it lowering the status of women, or increasing the domestic burdens of some members of the family? Does it result in diminished care for children through the dispersal of relatives formerly residing together? What types of house construction are envisaged: how is a house to be constructed, by whom, and when owned? What will the effect of new residence and housing patterns be on reproductive behavior?

It should be possible to estimate how long social change will take within a two-week period by examining other resettlement projects.

IRRIGATION PROJECTS

Two types of irrigation projects are of concern: the first involves the opening of new lands; the second, the improvement of access to available water. The degree of control and coordination required from all who are associated with such projects is exceptional. The engineering required to ensure the proper and timely supply of water is of an exacting nature, and the maintenance required is no less difficult. The social problems are of equal complexity. An adequate inventory of cultural resources is very important.

Rights to water have usually gone hand-in-hand with the development of sophisticated legal systems to regulate those rights. These legal systems are part of the wider system of social control, and they need to be thoroughly understood. Primarily, they regulate access that springs mainly from one's position in society. Any alterations of the existing social control of access to water must be closely regarded.

Benefit incidence requires special attention. Changes in access to water frequently alter the social position of one or more individuals, giving them a preeminent position and an ability to control others that was not traditionally their right. Very often the social consequences of redistribution have not been fully studied. Because irrigation projects demand such close social control, one concern is with utilization of existing institutions, both in the supervision and the collection of such charges as may be levied, as well as arrangements made for maintenance. Such data can usually be collected within two weeks.

Of more basic concern is the question of whether the resources provided will actually be used. There are instances of tube wells in India and irrigation schemes in Iran and Thailand where dams have been constructed but the waters are unused. The form of agriculture—disciplined coordination, residence requirements, relative inelasticity in terms of production—are all facts of life that have been mastered only after many centuries of experience by hydraulic communities. Therefore, this type of project requires thorough evidence that the social calculations are correct (see Table 6.4).

TABLE 6.4

Improved Water Supply, Upper Volta

To reduce the incidence of water-borne diseases in northern Upper Volta a number of wells were to be constructed by AID. Existing wells, while useful, tended to silt up. Deeper well construction was planned. However, similar projects executed in other areas of the Sahel had experienced severe problems.

When water supplies were improved in North Mali more cattle were introduced into the area. Despite attempts to get villagers to follow improved range management, overgrazing and destruction of grasslands resulted. Improving water supplies was not a technological problem but rather a social one.

Learning from previous experience in West Africa, the AID project studied the social landscape—social groups, social organization, mobility patterns—in order to decide on the optimum location of wells. By dispersing the wells over a wide geographical area rather than augmenting existing village supplies, overgrazing was prevented. Anticipation through analysis of social dimensions was important.

Source: Compiled by the author.

IMPROVED LIVESTOCK PROJECTS

Projects to improve livestock form a major part of agricultural project work. In many parts of the world, traditional methods of animal husbandry are inimical to the establishment of modern methods of livestock management. Initial inquiries relate to the social significance of the animals: are some sacred, as in India, or is possession an indication of social status, as among the Masai? What is the relationship between the social system of keeping animals and the kinds of changes called for with improved husbandry? Some want to sell cattle, some want to increase herd size and, thereby, their prestige, and some, like the Nilotic Nuer, may want to keep animals and drink their blood.

A second point of interest concerns the ownership of livestock. Does ownership rest with men, women, groups, or even with the gods? What are the group or individual rights regarding the ownership, maintenance, and consumption of livestock? Do these rights rest in one person or group to the exclusion of other individuals or groups, or are they dispersed through the society? What happens to cattle when they die or are slaughtered—are they a source of protein for the community? If so, are there important questions of taste to be taken into consideration? How are decisions made about castration, calving, the relationship between the number of cattle and pasture resources? What food resources are required for animal husbandry and what are the consequences of improvements in these factors?

Have opportunities for change been correctly identified and is it possible to mount extension programs that take these concerns into account? What is the relationship between access to grazing or water and the improvements? Is improvement in livestock leading to a diminution of other rights locally considered important? What is the pattern of inheritance? Is cattle ownership a significant factor in the relationship between generations? All of these factors will be important in determining appropriate communications strategies. This can usually be accomplished within a two-week period.

NUTRITION PROJECTS

Nutrition projects sometimes suffer from the same problems as population projects in that misunderstanding can arise between technical personnel with biochemical training and social scientists. Nutrition projects have sometimes found it difficult to stop distributing food in favor of increasing local capacity to produce a supply of nutritious food.

Food patterns are deeply ingrained in most communities and often associated with intricate systems of religious belief or social standing and status. Introduction of new foods or even selection of traditional foods for fortification needs to be done with care and, as with population projects, the progress of nutrition projects must be carefully observed to ensure that initial design assumptions are valid and that unforeseen participant reactions do not threaten project success. The following issues should receive attention:

What is the social meaning of food? What is the place of a particular type of food in a community? Is it associated with sickness or health, with feast or famine? Is it associated with old or young people? Do the wealthy people and the poor both eat it? Does the food have a religious or ritual significance?

What is the system for food distribution and food preparation? Do men get the largest share? Is there some logic behind the method of apportionment within families? Is food prepared in a way that results in a loss of valuable nutrients? Can the food be stored for long periods so that a balanced supply is available?

Are taste and preparation characteristics important? Do the new food types meet important taste needs in the community and can they be used in traditional recipes? Are the food types introduced related to those that can be produced locally? If food is grown, will it reach the right people in sufficient quantity?

POPULATION PROJECTS

Population projects often reinforce the idea that a major difficulty in implementation comes not from project participants but from officials. Medical and social science personnel traditionally have had different approaches, philosophies, and ways of working. Policy issues are also far from clear since some countries want to increase population while others want to reduce population growth sharply.

Reproductive issues—conception, spacing between children, abortion, and so on—are potentially explosive and devisive: population projects are among the most sensitive undertaken. It is therefore necessary, as early as possible during the implementation process, to ensure that initial design calculations are accurate. The following questions are designed to identify commonly encountered problems:

Have the advantages and disadvantages of not having children been correctly identified? Are children a form of insurance against old age? Are children an indication of womanhood so that to be barren carries a heavy social penalty? Do men feel social pressure to have children as an indication of virility? Are men and women who die childless thought to be more dead than those who leave children behind?

How is a decision to limit family size reached? Is it a decision that can be made by women alone? Is it a joint decision of husbands and wives? Does the project recognize the decision-making context?

Is the method of birth control convenient? Is it understood by men and women? Is there a possibility of pain or discomfort as a result of using this method? Is there a cost factor involved that may limit adoption? Is literacy a key factor in reproductive behavior?

Are project personnel able to establish rapport with clients? Is it easy for personnel to talk to women? Does the local indigenous system of medicine treat reproductive behavior?

Is the media campaign handling the right kinds of incentives and controls? Is the reaction favorable?

EDUCATION PROJECTS

An inventory of cultural resources is a necessary prerequisite to education project identification. The language of instruction, the nature of instructional technology, the social position and attitudes of the teacher are all important. Equally important are the process whereby pupils are selected, the forces that tend to encourage or discourage attainment of individual goals, the opportunity costs for individuals, the attitudes of parents, the location of the schools, and the kinds of things taught.

Education projects are not only concerned with the transmission of culture but also presuppose planners' conceptions of a future state of society. Institutional barriers to educational reform must be viewed in an attempt to spell out the value conflicts involved; for example, in many countries the educational system teaches that the highest expression of cultural values is found in careers in government, the church, or the army.

Reform of such a system may have to address itself to the problem of inculcating attitudes and values more conducive to business and commercial expansion. The same is true in the rural areas. One must calculate the potential for social change inherent in proposed educational reforms.

This leads to an assessment of the social realism involved in educational planning against the background of that society's beliefs and values. The question becomes "Education for What?" Is the system satisfying local aspirations in addition to producing people who are motivated to work in certain key positions? Will they remain in those positions for some time? What are the structural consequences of the system with respect to creation of new roles, effects on social stratification, and results in terms of newly emergent forms of access to power and status? Is there a good fit between the educational environment and the social environment, or is the system producing too many people for the limited number of positions available?

With formal education there is a more or less captive audience, a fair degree of consensus among administrators and administered about what education is or ought to be, a definite time period for instruction, a possibility for feedback, and an assumed motivation to learn on the part of the student.

Are educational goals meaningful to participants? Since the traditional classroom situation is not usually replicable on the desired scale, there is often heavy use of mass media. These can serve to focus attention and raise aspirations while at the same time indicating the means for achieving wish fulfillment. This being the case, it is axiomatic that media messages have a good cultural fit. The need for continuous monitoring and adjustment is a first requirement.

How is knowledge passed on and who is responsible for this process? What are the aims and objectives of traditional education? Who is responsible for what kinds of instruction? Is instruction by example, by practice, through discussion, or writing? What are the rules for participation with respect to age, sex, parental constellation, or belief? New programs must be grafted in attempts to introduce entirely new and untested forms of instruction.

The following issues must be considered in an evaluation of formal education programs:

What are the social characteristics of actual or potential pupils in terms of sex, age, parental constellation, religion, and ethnic or tribal origin? What are the mechanisms making for exclusion or inclusion of particular groups?

What are the social characteristics of the teachers, with regard to the language of instruction and their likely attitudes toward a selected series of occupations and roles?

In the case of nonresidential institutions, what is the degree of reinforcement attained by different home backgrounds during nonschool periods? Are instruction methods culturally relevant or failing to minimize the development of potentials?

Does content analysis of instruction methods indicate the existence of value conflicts or tend to downgrade use of training in occupations considered key in economic development?

What processes and influences are at work when students select their careers? Is choice primarily a result of access to particular kinds of information, the example of parents and peer group, teacher attitudes, or media presentations?

What are the structural consequences—creation of new social distinctions based on education attainment—of education for new jobs? What are the socially conceived components of job success, and is it possible to attach these components to sectors of the economy with a demand for high-level manpower? What does it mean to be illiterate or without education in urban and rural areas?

What are the political consequences of education for tribal or religious tensions? Is education seen as a way to promote national integration? What are the consequences of promoting denominational education?

What is the relationship between new methods and traditional forms of instruction; is too great a break presupposed? Is it possible to reform and build on the traditional methods?

What is the local perception of education in terms of what it should do, who it should provide for, what should be taught, how it should be financed and controlled? Is the system responsive, or can it be made so?

The following issues must be considered in an evaluation of nonformal education programs:

What are the social characteristics of the audience? Is instruction or advice being directed to the right groups and the right people in these groups? Is the traditional division of labor appreciated, and the social motivations behind that division? Is the message too broad in its design to have necessary local impact?

What is the actual or assumed motivation on the part of recipients? Is instruction relevant enough to focus attention and raise aspirations? Is regional or tribal variation required?

Are both the time allotted and the place of instruction conducive to success?

Is the message cognitively relevant and is it likely to be understood by the average person in the target area? Does it pay sufficient attention to what people already know and feel about the subject matter?

Where media are employed, have the right kinds of media been used and is there sufficient provision for feedback? Has the message a good balance between repetition and demonstration to ensure learning and yet prevent boredom?

Has attention been paid to the need for development of community associations and the importance of seeking their advice? Does the message take into account existing forms of organization and ways of doing things?

What is the local perception of media—are they thought to be unduly political or biased? Can media succeed although necessary backup and supporting organizations fail, thus imperiling future work?

Where local people are to be trained as teachers, has sufficient attention been paid to ensuring that they possess the requisite personal characteristics and social backgrounds for access to all members of their community after training? (See discussions of "Proximity" and "Measurement" in Chapter 5.)

ROAD PROJECTS

Often only minimal attention is paid to cultural impact of road projects because roads are seen as having considerable economic appeal and because the design and implementation of road projects are generally considered engineering problems. Many engineers feel that the need for roads is so great that any road, no matter where located, will bring sizable benefits.

Roads pose other interesting problems. One is the fact that, once a decision is made on the location of a road, issues of participation are not as important as in other types of projects: people living in the project area will be affected by the impact of a road project whether they like it or not. Project managers therefore have a special responsibility to identify in the fullest way possible the stream of costs and benefits that will be created by a road project, to ensure that full advantage is taken of the benefits and that full precautions are taken to ameliorate the negative consequences of road construction to the extent possible.

Another problem concerns the location of roads. Since the effects of roads normally extend nine to twelve kilometers from the roadbed, a location decision should be based on needs of suitable beneficiaries, as identified by the inventory of cultural resources. Normally, however, location is decided by a combination of engineering requirements and political pressure.

When the matter of location has been decided, attention can turn to three problem areas that account for most of the costs and benefits associated with road projects. These are land, labor, and services. Careful attention needs to be paid to the pattern of land utilization beside planned roads. A positive effect is that productivity may be increased because of the introduction of new crop types, provision of easier access to markets, and more readily available agricultural advice. On the negative side, land may become more precious and scarce, excessive fragmentation of plots may take place, and there may be pressure to register lands held under traditional tenure in the names of single owners. Family members who must leave their home areas and go to towns as a consequence of this registration process constitute a cost to the project. Litigation in local courts may increase over lands located beside roads.

Many of these problems can be prevented by a suitable land utilization plan. Such a plan must recognize the tendency to alter traditional cultivation cycles beside roads. Road construction can result in a loss of food crops, as a consequence of substituting cash crops, and a loss of fertility because land beside the roads no longer goes through the traditional fallow cycle.

There is increasing emphasis on labor-intensive road projects. Among the important considerations here are the manner of recruitment and the relationship of the technology employed to normal work patterns. Where there are large numbers of unemployed, attention must be paid to some locally acceptable method of job distribution. This can be done on a geographical basis; that is, those living in a particular district are employed when the road is constructed in their district. When construction moves to another area, the people of that district are given jobs. The disadvantage resides in the need to train new groups instead of accumulating skills.

The ways in which construction gangs are organized and the kinds of methods and techniques they use for road construction should, as far as possible, fit in with normal work patterns. If this is not done, construction may take longer, cost more, and may fail to leave many permanent contributions of value to the community. Skills learned during road construction should benefit the community when construction has been completed. Data on organizational factors can usually be collected within a month by experienced personnel.

With respect to the provision of services—medical, educational, agricultural—it is necessary to identify positive and negative aspects so that these can be treated by project design. In what ways will the access of poor people be widened

TABLE 6.5

Time and Cost[a] Estimates for Data Requirements

Type of Data	Components	Time in Man-months	Cost (dollars)
Cultural resources and human needs (Chapter 3)	1 Social mapping	6	30,000
	2 Social organization	6	30,000
	3 Belief systems	4	20,000
	4 Wealth forms	4	20,000
	5 Patterns of mobility	4	20,000
	6 Access to basic human needs	8	40,000
	Subtotal	32	160,000
If foregoing is available, the following times can be as follows:			
Project design (Chapter 4)	7 Spread effects	½	2,500
	8 Motivation	½	2,500
	9 Estimating time factors	½	2,500
	10 Benefit incidence	½	2,500
	11 Communication	1	5,000
	12 Using indigenous organization	1	5,000
	Subtotal	4	20,000
Project implementation (Chapter 5)	13 Critical behavioral factors	1	5,000
	14 Project close-out[b]	—	—
	15 Measurement[b]	—	—
	Total	37+	185,000

[a]Based on foreign expert probable costs.
[b]Depends on project life.

Note: The larger the country, the better the existing data base.

Source: Compiled by the author.

or narrowed as a consequence of road construction? In many instances, motorized visitation will become common in place of foot patrols. This can mean that fewer service personnel will be in villages overnight so that those who work all day in the fields may not receive attention. There may be reluctance among service personnel to visit inland because of a feeling that those wanting services should visit roadside stations. Critical behavioral factors of this type can be collected in about one month (see Table 6.5).

NOTES

1. Useful advice is to be found in Donald P. Warwick and Charles A. Lininger, *The Sample Survey: Theory and Practice* (McGraw-Hill, 1975).

2. United Nations, Research Institute for Social Development, *Contents and Measurement of Socio-Economic Development: A Beneficial Inquiry* (New York: Praeger, 1972).

3. For a good discussion, see Samuel L. Payne, *The Art of Asking Questions* (Princeton, N.J.: Princeton University Press, 1951); Frank Lynch, *Field Data Collection in Developing Countries*, report no. 10 (New York: Agricultural Development Council, 1976).

4. Village studies have a long tradition in India. See Michael Lipton and Michael Moore, *Village Studies in LDC's*, I.D.S. discussion paper (Sussex, England: Institute for Development Studies, n.d.).

5. Conrad M. Arensberg and Solon Kimball, *Culture and Community* (Gloucester, Mass.: Peter Smith, 1965). The anthropological method of data collection begins with the consideration of a broad number of facts and proceeds to the selection of a particular hypothesis, that is, the facts suggest the theory. Economists, however, begin with a hypothesis or certain assumptions, for example, perfect competition. The scientific method of economics is inductive. This distinction is argued in a fascinating exchange between the economist Frank H. Knight and the anthropologist Melville Herskovits, published in *Journal of Political Economy* 44, no. 2 (April 1941).

6. Author's paper "The Case for Fieldwork by Officials," *Man* 6, no. 2 (June 1971), discusses these problems.

7. I first heard this argument at a conference at Uppsala, Sweden. Later, while working in Morocco, I talked with people who admitted that allowance should be made for Berber populations in that country, though they said that this would be difficult in political terms.

8. A classic account of this is to be found in Morris Carstairs's book, *The Twice Born* (Bloomington: Indiana University Press, 1958), which describes a physician's attempts to move between Brahmin and untouchable children in the same village.

9. See Glynn Cochrane, "Land Tenure: The Case for Traditionalists," *Oceania* 65, no. 2 (December 1974); and "Choice of Residence in the Solomons and a Focal Land Model," *Journal of the Polynesian Society* 78, no. 3 (September 1961).

10. An excellent discussion is found in Ernest McLeod Dowson and Vivian Lee Dasborne Sheppard, *Land Registration* (London: Her Majesty's Stationery Office, 1956).

11. See *Mass Media in an African Context* (Paris: UNESCO, 1974), an evaluation of Senegal's Pilot Project, prepared by Henry R. Cassirer from H. de Jong and others.

12. Glynn Cochrane, "The Administration of Wagina Resettlement Scheme," *Human Organization* 29, no. 2 (1973).

7 INFRASTRUCTURE FOR DATA MANAGEMENT

Data collection for cultural appraisal should be accomplished within a year. Project managers will not themselves be primarily responsible for data collection. Instead, they will arrange for data collection, and evaluate and interpret data as they are produced. A strategy for data collection should begin with an inventory of existing cultural resources in order to estimate which can provide the kinds of data called for by the social dimensions of projects. The same methodology used in projects can be useful, that is, definition of groups and so on. Social science faculties at local universities, colleges, and training institutions should be assessed together with all other groups possessing distinctive information collection and interpretation capacity. Overseas resources should be examined next. With respect to organizational issues, what kinds of institutional resources are already available? Should grants be used to expand capacity in certain areas?

Without a strategy for collecting macrolevel social data to complement macrolevel economic data, wastage and error are inevitable. The social scientist asked to advise on a project must try to select the kinds of data required of an inventory of cultural resources and human needs before going on to tackle design and implementation issues. Since different social scientists are employed on different projects, duplication is inevitable. It is more likely that the real nature of poverty will not be determined and that, due to lack of information, project design will be faulty. Location of the project may also be poor.

A lack of macrolevel social data is more serious when important design decisions are being made because cultural factors that should be part of project design may be ignored or, if thought important, may be considered too late in the project cycle. This creates a situation in which cultural factors are "added in" as if they were extrinsic variables; thus, design cannot adequately anticipate positive and negative cultural factors.

Since information functions are not markedly different from economic functions, they can usefully be examined to see if they are contextual and incremental. For example, questionnaire surveys have long been used in India: to attempt the same thing in Burma would probably be disastrous because Burma has fewer people with the required skills. Statistical interpretations should be incremental, otherwise there is a danger that, when introduced, they will have minimal spread effects. Therefore, any attempt to improve the information resources should begin by assessing the functions of central government, local government, and the academic community. Following this, contracting and research needs can be assessed.

GOVERNMENT STRUCTURES

It is the author's view that the collection and analysis of the types of information required for the cultural appraisal of projects must increasingly become a local government responsibility in developing countries. Improvement of resources for government collection and analysis of data can be viewed in terms of "centralization" versus "decentralization."[1] In centralized systems, powers, duties, and responsibilities are concentrated in the capital; with decentralized systems the reverse is true. Information gathering, analysis, and discrimination functions are embedded in the relationship between the center and the field. There are, however, disadvantages to this kind of dichotomy. Discussion of decentralization implies that things are being transferred from the center to rural areas. Yet it is not true that the center and the field are equally suitable locations for similar sorts of powers, duties, and functions: the powers, duties, and responsibilities of central and local government are different. Treatment of information will also differ.

With respect to information, which powers, duties, and responsibilities are best exercised at the center, which in the field? In some instances—for example, customs or national defense—decentralization is not really plausible. It is often clear that the center must have responsibility for national policy making and allocation of scarce resources. But local government regulations and bylaws can only be made at the local level.

All government activities can be classified on a departmental basis into control or extension departments. Those responsible for control would be (national) police, judicial, audit, posts and telecommunications, and so on; decentralization is not relevant to most of their work. There is broad agreement on how such departments obtain and use information. Those responsible for extension might be agriculture, health, education, and so on. Devolution or, more important, decentralization is necessary for such departments. Controlling departments administer nationally determined decisions in local areas and exercise a minimum of personal discretion. The personnel associated with such departments may serve in local areas and coordinate their activities with local officials but they will, in the main, answer to central authority.

With extension departments, the question is more difficult. Within the national guidelines the question of which information functions are to be carried out locally, and how these are to be accomplished, is a matter for local determination. The sharing of responsibility is between the central government, which may indicate broadly what is to be done, using as positive and negative sanctions, legal penalties, and financial incentives, and local government, which must plan and implement to suit the local context.

The object of creating more genuinely democratic structures at the local level is not simply to promote economic development or to obtain maximum citizen participation (it is, after all, known that many people in industrial societies do not participate in elections—to use this as a test of the viability of democracy might be dangerous). The need is to create a multipurpose information framework that enables local people to plan, execute, and review a wide variety of activities. Local government must become responsible for more and more project work. For example, what is taught in local schools, whether education should be the same for boys and girls, what is the best emphasis in agricultural planning, what should the nature of health care be—all these issues are best settled at the local level.[2] And it is at the local level also that the best chance is to be found for the identification and alleviation of the problems of the poorest.

The means of achieving the best mix of powers, duties, and responsibilities between field and center for information needs is not to divide up what already exists but to look at the overall allocation of powers and then make the new allocation. Many developing countries have incorrect ministerial portfolios; many should completely reorganize their ministerial structures. Reorganizing local government information functions on the assumption that the center is correctly organized will often be self-defeating.

Colonialism initially concentrated all significant information, powers, duties, and responsibilities at the center (district administration personnel were agents of the central government). As the competence and capacity of local governments increased they were, year by year, given more responsibility. The aim would, ultimately, have been an adequate division; however, in many countries this process was arrested at the time of independence. Postindependence activity often reversed the trend to stronger local government, strengthening central government instead. In some instances, so little was known of the real meaning and nature of local government that district administration personnel were considered part of local government.

The search for a methodology to deal with local government would be barren if it were not part of a larger exercise directed not only at the reorganization of all government activities and delineation of the distribution of powers, duties, and responsibilities but also at the identification of means of coordinating field and center activity and the extent to which local social patterns are explicitly recognized in any ensuing arrangements.[3]

Local Government Finance

Someone must pay for information functions. Few local government authorities have access to regular, substantial revenue and as a consequence their development activities and the quality of personnel that they can attract and retain suffer adversely. Forest products, minerals, trade, fishing, indirect taxation, custom tariffs, most direct taxation, and proceeds of international development assistance usually accrue to the central government in the first instance.[4]

Local governments obtain most of their revenue from licenses (firearms, radios, stores, and so on), from rental of facilities such as markets or abattoirs, from flat-rate taxes levied on all able-bodied males, and so on. The characteristics of local government finance are that the amounts are usually small, the administrative costs of tracking down those liable are heavy, and the incidence of improper avoidance is usually high. It is bad for confidence to know that many do not make their proper contributions. It is bad for morale of local government officials to know that a high proportion of what is collected goes for their personal emoluments.

Block grants are often given to local governments on a per capita basis or as a result of specific local government proposals made in answer to central government announcements of fund availability. The block grant has the disadvantage that money is often taken from the rural area and then brought back again, a process that throws a heavy strain on scarce administrative resources. On the other hand, the grant proposal method requires repeated application for specific sums and thus tends to favor the local authorities with large staffs possessing the necessary grantsmanship skills.

Obviously, the size of the tax base is a crucial issue. In many countries the size of local government reflects divisions suitable for purposes of colonialism, instead of reflecting economic factors. Extreme variation in size operates to the disadvantage of the smaller authorities—a minimum local government entity should probably be created by law.

Personnel

Information functions require sufficiently well-trained personnel. Colonial local government failed to manage staffing successfully. Third World countries have to live with this heritage. The most able people often wanted to join the central government. In all too many cases there was no unified local government service with comprehensive pensions and other benefits and provisions. It proved difficult to transfer local personnel from one authority to another. Those who were of local origin in a particular local authority were often too closely tied to kinsmen. It proved to be very difficult to get financial personnel to audit local government accounts. Often personnel who had been sent overseas on expensive training courses and had begun to make real progress were lured away by the higher salaries offered by private enterprise.

INFORMATION CONSTITUENCIES

Information means different things to different people in government. Therefore, it is important to delineate different information constituencies. Ministries will sometimes conceal information from each other; some kinds of information will be ignored or suppressed. Delineation of information constituencies is not simply a matter of mapping different groups, but of understanding the values responsible for their treatment of information.

Although many Third World universities are organized on interdisciplinary lines, it is important to appreciate the strength of traditional disciplinary interests. Academic communities have information constituencies like those found in government. Each discipline has its own values and beliefs, and solutions to problems are favored to the extent that they support the values and beliefs held important by the discipline.

Anthropology

The discipline of anthropology has been collecting data on poor people for over half a century, yet these resources are at present little used. Anthropologists can collect high-quality data and have considerable abilities for analysis of functional relations at the local level. The discipline contains specialists in population, nutrition, education, and rural development; an increasing number of younger anthropologists are interested in practical careers. If consulted early enough, they can offer very valuable insights on most of the steps outlined in the chapter on project design.

Anthropologists have tended to shy away from involvement in governmental affairs; thus, organizational experience is rarely available in the teaching institutions, which has affected the discipline's views and attitudes. Basic textbooks still show little awareness of contemporary development policies, problems, and practices. Teamwork, as in most other disciplines, is not very strong, demographic and quantitative skills are not emphasized, and little attention is paid to communications media. Anthropologists have concentrated on first-hand, person-to-person contacts.

The practical consequences of this situation is that numbers of anthropologists would be required to help with countrywide or regional social mapping, because the real strength of the discipline is at the village level. Ideally, anthropologists should be given a period for learning about organizational requirements before being given assignments. On the other hand, they are expert at data collection and should, if possible, be asked to evaluate data collection.

It is advisable to draw up a roster of anthropologists for a whole country or region where projects are to be carried out. The number included in the roster should permit geographical as well as functional (for example, education projects, nutrition, and so on) coverage. When this roster is being drawn up, care should be exercised to record the extent of each anthropologist's experience with project work. It is also wise to ensure that each anthropologist on a roster is basically in sympathy with the known philosophical assumptions underlying project work. Development is, after all, a political process and some anthropologists participate quite vigorously in that process.[5]

Economics

Economists have considerable strengths and weaknesses for project work. Strengths stem from several decades of highly successful leadership in project work in developing countries, the fruits of which have filtered back into teaching in the universities. The simple vigor of project calculations is a testimony to the common sense approach of economists and their ability to focus on the essentials of a problem. Given their strong quantitative skills, economists can, in addition to normal financial and economic analysis, give valuable help in disaggregating national figures and statistics and in estimating benefit incidences, project impact, and spread effects.

Economists usually have no firsthand experience of social conditions in remote rural areas of developing countries. Where they have experience as economists in developing countries has usually been in regional urban areas or the capital. Economists are usually not interdisciplinary and too few take the trouble to see what other social scientists can do.[6] A common problem among economists involves their tendency to adopt an oversimplified view of positive and negative incentives to production, an approach sometimes revealed in the attitude of economists who believe that a problem that has not been quantified is a problem not yet sufficiently thought through. As with anthropology, a consultant roster should be drawn up.

Geography

Geographers are in some ways similar to anthropologists, especially if they call themselves "human geographers." Human geographers undertake fieldwork—their real expertise lies in handling spatial relationships. In this connection, they perform valuable work in mapping—in working out the location of projects and the probability of achieving spread effects. Geographers can also contribute to an understanding of the relationship between society, culture, and environment insofar as these concepts are related to incremental and contextual considerations as described in the chapter on project design. Geographers usually have had good quantitative training.

Modern geography involves a considerable degree of specialization, something that is only natural in a discipline trying to span the gap between the physical and social sciences. Economic and human geographers will usually be useful in project work. They will, however, generally be of more utility at the macrolevel than at the microlevel. Geography as a discipline is more oriented toward planning — land use rather than land tenure — than implementation.[7] Though there may be individual exceptions, geographers as social scientists are not well suited to the study of motivation, beliefs, attitudes, and values as they are to the design and evaluation of organizational structures.

Political Science

Development is a political process and political scientists have a great deal of useful information about how things happen as a result of events in the political arena. They are particularly adept at analyzing how development programs can gain and maintain support, how institutions can be strengthened, and what the role of factions and minority groups is likely to be. As such they can do valuable work on matters such as delineation of groups, leadership, benefit incidence, and identification of obstacles.

Much of this work, however, has been concentrated on national politics at the expense of the local level. This concentration does not illuminate the position of the poorest, many of whom do not participate in national or even regional political life. Attempts to build models, use statistics, define modernization processes, and so on have usually added a good deal to the basic phenomena being studied. In the past, too few political scientists have been trained in obtaining high-quality data at the village level. This position is changing and an increasing number of political scientists should be able to offer valuable assistance on questions involving local government and its relationship with central government.[8]

Public Administration

The traditional concerns of public administration with management, budgeting, and personnel have now been augmented by a concern with analysis of public policy. Past interest in local government of developing countries has died away and most work in the last few years has centered on large public bureaucracies. Public administration specialists know how these organizations should be run and how people can be trained to run them. They also have skills in what has been called "institution building" and the devising of management information systems to fit local capacity. Since the contribution of public service to development is vital, public administration specialists are important people whose views should be considered at both the mapping and the project design stages.

One weakness of public administration involves the fact that many graduates have little administrative experience. Because the subject matter—public institutions, civil servants, and their responsiveness to the public will—is by nature interdisciplinary, there is a certain theoretical self-consciousness among public administration teachers. This self-consciousness results in frequent self-examination and attempts to gain academic respectability by what can be called "sciencing," for example, using theories and computers in a way that sounds good but really helps understanding very little.

Specialization can be a weakness of public administration since what distinguishes the good public administrator is humanity and an encompassing grasp of societal matters, combined with an ability to see relationships and possibilities where others see none. If management is wanted, the answer is to be found among the graduates of business schools; if quantitative methods are wanted, the answer is to be found among statisticians and econometricians; if policy analysis is required, the answer is to be found among political scientists; and if one wishes to see how these elements combine to lift performance in the public service, the answer ought to lie with public administrators.[9]

Social Psychology

Social psychologists have good quantitative skills and an increasing number are capable of collecting high-quality data at the local level. They can play a very valuable role in handling data about local perceptions of development and poverty, motivations for change or nonchange, appropriate role behavior, and ways in which people learn to innovate. These factors are potentially of great importance to population, nutrition, and education projects. It is vital that more social psychologists become associated with projects at the earliest possible moment.

Because social psychology has little field data of value on record, there is often delay because requests can only be met through new research. Social psychologists are usually better working with microlevel problems. Most social psychological research has been executed with research, rather than operational, requirements foremost in mind. The most operationally relevant work has been done in the communications field (for example, what do figures and symbols on posters mean in other cultures—what do size, shape, color, and form convey to a cross-cultural audience?).[10] These posters have been used in several countries to promote health and agricultural development programs.

The great strength of most social psychologists is that they have good quantitative training and can perform well in questionnaire surveys. Furthermore, they do not require excessive amounts of time to carry out their fieldwork.

Sociology

Sociologists have good quantitative skills and have worked well with economists in recent years. They can perform valuable service at the mapping stage and at all stages of project design. They have the capacity to obtain high-quality data. They are problem- and issue-oriented and are used to giving judgments and opinions. They are also capable of carrying out original research within a reasonably short period of time.[11]

Most of what has been said about anthropology also applies to sociology. The difference between the two is that generally the former has been attracted to problems in developing countries while the latter has concentrated on problems in industrial countries. The practical consequence of this is that sociologists usually have, during their training, been less exposed to data from developing countries than have anthropologists. Though the problems chosen by an anthropologist and sociologist may differ in nature and setting, the methods and techniques used in analysis are similar. Many anthropologists, however, call themselves sociologists because of the feeling in many developing countries that having an anthropologist study one's society implies that the society is primitive.

CONTRACTING WITH INSTITUTIONS

When information needs have been assessed, contracts may be given to suitable institutions. The capacity of academic institutions, particularly where universities in industrial countries are concerned, is very difficult to estimate, and great care should be taken to study an institution before scarce resources are committed to contracts that may benefit the institution more than the government. Many academic institutions have a good deal of window dressing: they may have well-known academics on board and may obtain visibility from a few high-level studies, but most of the day-to-day business and research is carried out by low-level people. A weakness of many research institutes is that not only are they unwilling or unable to commit their best people but often their best people have good academic reputations and all too little practical experience. Unless employment of persons known to have practical experience is stipulated, or the project manager himself has access to someone with extensive academic experience, contracting may be a most dangerous business.

A contract for mapping or project design should be given only after soliciting proposals from a number of institutions. Part of this may be a psychological problem arising because these may be the project manager's former teachers, part may be due to the idea that institutes and universities are nonprofit organizations. Academics do go through the equivalent process when they apply to research grants. A competitive process is the most satisfactory way of awarding research contracts.

Governments also have an interest in developing research capacity so that it can continually be drawn upon. The information needs of a country, both in the short and the long term, may suggest the advisability of an institution building grant.[12]

Consultants

When a countrywide or regional inventory of cultural resources and human needs is completed, and this should be accomplished within a year, attention can turn to project work. A first step is to assess the nature and scope of project operations planned for the next five-to-ten-year period (or within national plan limits if this is different). This can be broken down on a sectoral and regional basis, that is, transport or population projects in the north and south. This will establish the nature and scope of projects to be carried out. Cultural appraisal data can then be identified and the rosters for various disciplines can be consulted. Thereafter, if a nutrition project is contemplated in a locale, it should be possible to contact someone with the appropriate kind of expertise. When that individual has finished, a report on her or his work should be kept. The inventory of future project work should be matched by an inventory of individuals with the necessary skills to work on such projects (see Table 7.1).

Consultant Management

Construction of a roster of capable individuals does present some problems. Not every well-known academic is suited to project work. Teamwork, the subordination of self in favor of common enterprise, and the capacity to take a backseat on occasion are qualities and attributes not always highly rewarded in university life. Where an individual's technical contribution to a project is seen as vital, something about his or her personal outlook and bureaucratic ability must be known well in advance of the award of an assignment.

The most economical way of managing social science consultants is to assume that the relationship between project staff and academics or consultants is to be long-term and mutually beneficial. A first step before any specific assignments are given is to ensure that the individuals being considered for assignments are given an opportunity to learn about organizational procedures and practices. The object of such familiarization is ensuring that those who are being considered know what kinds of data are required in projects, what kinds of judgments and opinions are needed, and when these things must be accomplished. Anyone accepting an assignment from an organization without knowing its absorptive capacity is unwise. The best report in the world is only as good as the capacity of those who receive it to translate it into an organizationally relevant document.

TABLE 7.1

Sample Consultant Roster Form

Name ——————————————— Telephone ———————————

Mailing address ————————————————

Sex   M ——— F ——— Nationality ———————— Language proficiency

Current position (with address) —————————————————————

Major publication(s) and/or positions held in other organizations/governments

Functional speciality (for example, rural development, nutrition, population, and the like)

Geographic expertise (for example, northeast Thailand)
  (a) Primary area ——————————————————
  (b) Secondary area(s) —————————————

Previous project-related experience —————————————————

Suitability for short-term assignments (for example, personality, ability to produce reports under deadlines) ————————————————————

Ability to coordinate with other specialists (for example, knowledge of other fields, teamwork, willingness to accept direction and supervision) —————————————————

Availability information (time of year when available, amount of prior notice, and the like)

Source: Compiled by the author.

A second step for officials writing descriptions of the scope of work for consultants is to become familiar with the ways in which universities, institutes, or consultant firms operate. They need to know the kinds of research carried out, the kind of writing usually done, what the rewards and penalties are, and so on. Contracting for social science expertise has to be a bilateral affair in which each party gets something of value and each tries to accommodate the other's needs and desires.

The final step in the precontracting process is a meeting to discuss the nature of the assignment. Here the project manager needs to demonstrate that he or she has clear, substantive areas in mind and a firm series of expectations. The project manager should stress that the format of the report must address already identified categories and frameworks, for example, steps presented in the chapters on inventory of cultural resources and project design. In addition, the specific possibilities suggested by the project type checklists can be referred to, and highlighted during, discussion.

The actual timing and nature of the work output should also be discussed at this time so that both parties are quite clear about what is required and when. Of course, it is not always possible to settle all items at the precontract stage. Where fieldwork, quantitative surveys, or original research are involved, it is well to allow six months to a year. Where the data are already available or the researcher is familiar with the area, three months will probably suffice. Some fieldworkers may insist that they need a year or two in the field, but this is not necessary where assignments are given on the basis of experience. The point of contracting is not to assist the universities in the training of new graduates—that takes years—but to employ those resources already created at public expense.

INSTITUTIONALIZING SOCIAL SCIENCE FOR DEVELOPMENT

The history of social science usage in U.S. development assistance illustrates some common problems. Anthropology provides a good example. Why, in 1974, in a country where some anthropologists are household names, was there no anthropological Ph.D. permanently employed by AID (or the World Bank)— and this at a time when development assistance was supposed to go to the poorest overseas? The emphasis on programs to reach those bypassed by previous development assistance called for the kinds of expertise that anthropologists possess.

It is almost 20 years since anthropologists and other noneconomic social scientists were first used by AID. The last usage was with community development programs during the 1950s and early 1960s. But, despite the fact that it is still prominent in the applied anthropology literature, community development was discarded because 20 years ago AID wanted to be able to measure the results of its development programs and the benefits of community development were viewed as too subjective, too imprecise. Economists were successful in persuading the U.S. Congress and AID that national income and growth are what matters. These developments can be quantified. The focus moved to the macrolevel and the microview of the anthropologist was no longer felt to be so important. The benefits of national growth would, economists felt, gradually trickle down to the poorest in the countries receiving development assistance. Anthropology had no obvious importance in the development thinking of the growth model era during the 1960s. The theory of development affected AID recruitment patterns: economists were recruited; anthropologists and other social scientists were not.

At the same time anthropologists were becoming increasingly disenchanted with the political aspects of development assistance. Simultaneously, expansion in university life of the 1960s made the campus very attractive. Thus, when AID did wish to hire anthropologists it faced difficult problems. Senior academics hired by AID were found to be too interested in working on their own areas of research interest. Lacking bureaucratic skills, they were often outmaneuvered in the annual fight for funds and staff. Disgusted, they returned to their universities. When junior anthropologists were hired, AID had supervision problems. Young anthropologists had to acquire the appreciated quantitative skills of their economist colleagues in order to survive and prosper in AID. Gradually, by the time they had managed to get promotions in AID, they ceased to operate as anthropologists. Any organization, if it is to use anthropologists, must use them at various levels and have training and career development plans geared to that speciality.

When development assistance policies changed in the early 1970s, the employment opportunity was not seized by anthropologists. Anthropologists, as professionals, had not kept up with the new thinking in development assistance. Population, education, nutrition, rural development, and so on were the preserve of a very few anthropologists. Too few introductory texts handled such issues.

Applied anthropology books and reports discussed anthropology in general. They did not focus on the specific problems faced by AID personnel who knew all too little anthropology: the reports were written to appeal to fellow academics. Insofar as they related to development problems, the reports used the favorite device of the applied anthropologist—showing how things had gone wrong through lack of attention to some cultural principle or other. But what AID wanted to know was, How do you employ cultural principles in order to successfully implement specific programs?

There are three strands to any strategy for successfully institutionalizing the social sciences for development. Step one involves creation of institutional demand for social science insights by ensuring that such inputs are called for during the project cycle. If personnel seeking project approval know that they must use social science methods and techniques in order to win approval, they begin to request personnel with those skills. The ability of those on the ground to identify the instances when social science can be useful, and which kind of social science is required, is critically important. The second strand is therefore concerned with creation of training courses to meet the demand for new social science skills. The third strand involves ensuring that an agency obtain its own permanent core of social science specialists to provide supporting services in the field.

Learning from Consulting Firms

If one compares the intellectual resources available to most universities and those available to medium-sized consulting firms in industrial countries, it is hard to see how many of the consulting firms specializing in social science survive. Of course, a few universities do not use their best faculty in fulfilling research contracts. However, this in itself is not a satisfactory explanation for the relative success of consulting firms. By and large, the universities do have better talent, but the consulting firms are reputed to turn in a more operationally relevant product.

Consulting firms begin by studying the client organization. They know what their clients can and cannot use. They do not feel the need to appear scholarly, to show intelligence or brilliance, or to rebut what so-and-so wrote a few years ago. They seem to be reasonably objective professionals at the job of meeting their clients' needs. Consulting firms adapt their staffs and organizational resources to the task at hand, without being bound by trade unionism or jurisdictional disputes.

Research Strategies

Frequently, research into such areas as reproductive behavior, agricultural credit, or education fails to have any impact on project designs. Many problems result from industrial countries' ethnocentric approach to research and development rather than Third World countries' reactions. One example of this is seen in the industrialized countries' stress on participation—the idea that development assistance projects should secure the maximum participation of the poorest citizens. In a sense the issue is wrongly stated: the issue is not to secure "their" participation in "our" projects, but is rather to justify "our" participation in "their" development.

The level of skills called for in particular development assistance projects must be related to the level of existing skills in a particular developing country rather than the level found in an industrial country that can produce a somewhat ideal solution. This draws attention to the fact that projects and program systems cannot usefully be drawn up at a global level. Project systems—even with useful global suggestions—must be designed to fit local capacity, otherwise dependency is increased.

The greatest obstacle to genuine participation is the fact that many development systems are so complicated that communities cannot gain confidence in their development ability: the systems introduced only work with the import of outside experts. Yet local communities need to gain confidence in their ability and capacity to manage their own affairs.

As a general proposition, it seems reasonable to suggest that any development system devised completely in industrial countries has a limited chance of success. Such an approach may wrongly imply that the brains are all in industrial countries, whereas research should be collaborative. Furthermore, local idiosyncrasies are part of the research and not something to be added in later. Research is not a privileged niche that is somehow exempt from the concept of collaboration. Research methodologies, like planning, must recognize the need to begin from the bottom and work up to the top.

Linkage: Operations and Research Manpower

Even allowing for a necessary time lag while research findings trickle down to projects and programs, it does seem clear that there is a wide gap between research and operations. The actual calculations made, for example, in the course of the World Bank's project cycle, have not changed significantly in the last decade.[13] Too little of such costly social science research becomes operational.

There must be a clearly stated linkage between the manpower capacity of the research organization and that of the development assistance or other organization that is supposed to implement the research. With each piece of research, the kinds of manpower skills that will be needed to operate the ideas must be specified; these skills should be compared with the existing inventory of manpower skills and early arrangements made to adjust for any shortfall. If a research team is made up of famous academics straining their brains and using all their skill to find an elegant solution, how will the research be operationalized?

IN-HOUSE CAPACITY

Some organizations operate under the assumption that their own permanent manpower core of skills is not vital to operational effectiveness, the logic being that the entire range of skills that might be required cannot possibly be used on a permanent basis. Unusual demands should be met through consultancy. It is better to get specialists on demand from the universities—they will be technically fresh.

Such a manpower utilization procedure, however, requires at least a minimum of in-house (that is, within an agency) capacity in the specialty in question. Without this minimum the agency usually does not even know where to look for a specialist. How can the terms of reference be drawn up? If there is no in-house capacity it is hard for the agency to know what the person in question actually can or cannot do. It is equally hard for the specialist to know what kinds of things the agency should be told.

The danger is that, through lack of in-house capacity, funds will be wasted and research duplicated. This has probably happened on numerous occasions. Weak, uneconomical research results are usually attributed to the weakness of researchers, instead of being attributed to the initial inefficiency of the people concerned with drawing up terms of reference in the agency.

Research Drafting to Operational Specifications

Social science research is too often carried out far from where operations are executed. Research should be drafted to meet operational specifications. For example, instead of always increasing general knowledge about income distribution a group of researchers could, on occasion, be required to develop their contribution and new methods and ways of handling income distribution, based on research findings, could be instituted so that not only the operation of the organization but also its level of performance would be permanently affected.

Researchers too often meet only their research counterparts in an organization. In fact, they should spend a great deal of time with those who will carry out the operations. However, one very seldom encounters operational people when agency and academic personnel hold conferences to discuss research matters.

Responsibility for Implementation

Most of those in organizations exercising oversight on behalf of agencies are not in an operational division. Many have never been in operations or have been away from the field for years. When a research contract is first envisaged, thought must be given to having one person associated with the research team and another associated with the development assistance agency, both of whom will be responsible for implementation of relevant research findings. It is too late to think about implementation when a contract is finished; research must be carried out with implementation firmly in mind. Project managers who are effective in implementing research findings are not overly concerned with whether a piece of work is economics or public administration—their sole concern is to get the job done well.

Universities, particularly in industrialized countries, are still organized along fairly medieval lines. Too few universities have a nutrition department truly integrated with the social sciences. Too few social science departments or development centers have agriculture integrated into their activities. Too few universities are organized along intellectual lines to produce the kinds of thinking that rural or urban development require.

CONCLUSIONS

Popular theories about development assistance produced in industrialized countries, and the policies that reflect those theories, have usually ignored idiosyncratic cultural factors. Projects with the emphasis on achieving economic growth and increases in productivity have been planned without sufficient attention having been paid to the cultural context of the society in which the projects were to be located. The recent adoption of a "basic needs" policy may not be helpful, since it contains assumptions about the nature of problems and their solutions in too superficial a manner. This is no less true for private voluntary organizations than it is for official assistance.

Cultural factors are still not handled systematically in development projects. The norms of many private and official development assistance organizations responsible for projects still stress spending of funds rather than achievement of social change. Lines of communication are still too long. Responsibility for the project cycle must be localized and the local people more involved in planning and executing their own projects. This is an important goal for those who recognize a need for participation in the planning process by the recipients of project assistance.

Identification of the possibilities for productive social change is vital to an improved project process. Cultural appraisal can be systematically carried out in an economic fashion. Regardless of which project beneficiaries are selected as a consequence of economic and political decision making, a national inventory of cultural resources and human needs is still necessary for project identification. The treatment of cultural factors at the project identification stage must be systematized. When an inventory has been constructed, it becomes possible to plan where it should be located and to estimate where benefits will be experienced. Without such an inventory, scarce resources may be wasted or not used to their maximum advantage, and such quantitative data as exist may be misunderstood. This is so because quantitative data on income, caloric intake, or education may mean very little to those not living in the project area unless complemented by information about the social circumstances of those concerned.

Project design can be molded to the social landscape of project participants in a systematic manner rather than molded to the intellectual landscape of planners. Project design must reflect the cultural context and can then provide a basis for the integration of the various forms of project analysis—the organizational, financial, economic, and so on.

Instead of each piece of analysis being separately undertaken, and separately evaluated, by project managers, it is possible to examine each of the criteria for cultural appraisal and then to have the different analyses address the same criteria. For example, organizational criteria, discussed in the chapters on project identification and project design, can be examined by an anthropologist (or a sociologist or social psychologist), by an economist undertaking economic analysis, or by a political scientist undertaking organizational analysis. Motivation criteria can be handled in the same manner.

Implementation to minimize costs and maximize performance requires that project managers have local discretion, a sound understanding of the range of possibilities for social change, and good sources of data. From a cultural appraisal perspective, the implementation phase has two lessons: the vital importance of project managers' analyses of the various dimensions of the social change process and the advisability of project managers undertaking small, manageable projects.

To create a suitable data base for the cultural appraisal of projects requires both funds and time, not an unreasonable investment, but, rather, one that can be shown to result in savings through production of better projects. For project managers, better data mean an increased ability to make timely project decisions.

It is not necessary for project managers to conceptualize "hard" and "soft" data. Hard data must be interpreted in cultural context, that is, they need a soft component to be fully comprehensible. Soft data need a hard component to be useful in project work. Project managers, using cultural appraisal, can focus attention on criteria that have both a quantitative and qualitative dimension. An excess of quantitative or qualitative data alone is likely to be misleading.

Project managers in the field need support from their headquarters. Most multilateral and bilateral development assistance organizations are not organized to carry out policies that emphasize reaching the poorest overseas, and they have provided Third World countries interested in the cultural appraisal of projects with few examples. Third World governments have undertaken their own initiatives. Consequently, disparity between the resources devoted by the major multilaterals and bilaterals to improving economic and technical analyses and those devoted to improving cultural analysis continues.

Progress has been made in AID but the World Bank still has 1,000 staff members with economic and business qualifications for every one staff member operating as an anthropologist or sociologist.

Because of the absence of a suitable cultural appraisal methodology, social scientists and project managers have remained at arm's length from each other. Social scientists have traditionally resisted giving "how-to-do-it" advice because, recognizing the complexity of cultural arrangements, they feared appearing to endorse what to them appeared to be simple, mechanical procedures that might do more harm than good. However, there is a fundamental difference between "how-to-do-it" kinds of guidance and cultural appraisal information aimed at increasing a project manager's awareness of "who-can-do-it." Project managers are, after all, the linchpin in the process of undertaking cultural appraisal. Decisions that project managers make—whether help is needed, what kind of help, and so on—will continue to determine standards in the cultural appraisal of projects.

The implications of this analysis for cultural appraisal are similar to the lesson anthropologists have learned from the study of culture. Cultural appraisal of development projects procedures must be holistic and must be undertaken comprehensively. Appraising individual projects with the kinds of data developed from an inventory of cultural resources or project design alone would be as misleading as the current practice that allows each social scientist to interpret the meaning of cultural appraisal.

New policies require new inputs. If the now popular development assistance policies continue to stress the need to reach the poorest developing countries (and there may well be argument or dispute with what is written here), there cannot be a denial of the need to explore such ideas on a more energetic basis.

> "Cheshire Puss," said Alice, "Would you please tell me which way I should go from here?"
> "That depends a good deal on where you want to get to," said the cat.
> "I don't much care where," said Alice.
> "Then it doesn't matter which way you go," said the cat.
> "—so long as I get somewhere," Alice added.
> "Oh you're sure to do that," said the cat, "if only you go far enough."[14]

NOTES

1. James W. Fesler, "Approaches to Understanding of Decentralization," *Journal of Politics* 27 (1965); Philip Mawhood, "Decentralization for Development—A Lost Cause?" *Local Politics, Development and Participation,* ed. Fred C. Bruhns, Franco Cazzola, and J. Wiatr (Pittsburgh: University Center for International Studies, 1974).

2. This is the approach adopted in a recent work by Edgar Faure and his associates, *Learning to Be* (Paris: UNESCO, 1972).

3. There are only passing references to local government these days. Not much has happened since Ursula Hicks published *Development from Below* in 1960. Journals considered to be influential have published very few articles on local government. *Economic Development and Cultural Change* has not had an article on the subject since 1973; the same is true of the *Journal of Development Studies.* The *Journal of Developing Areas* and the *Journal of Comparative Administration* have picked at the problem but with little enthusiasm. Local government is kept alive in most vigorous form in the *Journal of Administration Overseas.* This journal, a successor to the *Journal of African Administration,* was established to promote interest in local government and is sponsored by the Ministry of Overseas Devel-

opment. For a comprehensive survey, see "Special Issue on Research in Rural Africa," *Canadian Journal of African Studies* 3, no. 1 (1969).

4. See Ursula Hicks, *Development from Below* (Oxford: Clarendon Press, 1960).

5. Criticism of past training in schools of anthropology and suggestions for change are contained in the author's, *Development Anthropology* (New York: O.U.P., 1971); and *What We Can Do for Each Other* (Amsterdam: B. R. Gruner, 1976).

6. Kurt Martin and John Knoff, eds., *Manchester Conference on Teaching Economic Development* (London: Aldine, 1967).

7. Richard J. Chorley and Peter Haggert, eds., *Models in Geography* (London: London University Press, 1967).

8. Daniel Lerner and Wilbur Schramm, *Communications and Change in the Developing Countries* (Honolulu: East-West Center, 1967).

9. Fredrick C. Mosher, *American Public Administration: Past, Present, Future* (University: University of Alabama Press, 1975); Ralph A. W. Rhodes, *Current Developments in the Study of Public Administration in the United States* (Birmingham, England: University of Aston, 1976).

10. David C. McClelland, *The Achieving Society* (New York, 1961).

11. Seymour M. Miller and Alvin W. Gouldner, eds., *Applied Sociology* (New York, 1965).

12. *Report on 211 (d) Research Grants* (Washington, D.C.: AID, 1974) gives an outline of AID research funding and activities and the agency's future priorities. See also *Abstracts of Research* (Washington, D.C.: International Bank for Reconstruction and Development, 1976), containing a summary of the kinds of research activities sponsored by the World Bank (IBRD).

13. See, for example, Warren L. C. Baum, "The Project Cycle," *Finance and Development* 7, no. 2 (June 1970); James Price Gittinger, *The Economic Analysis of Agricultural Projects* (Baltimore: Johns Hopkins University Press, 1972). The kinds of calculations and levels of expertise called for by World Bank calculations are not markedly different from those to be seen in AID's *Project Manual* (Washington, D.C.: AID, 1974).

14. From Lewis Carroll's *Alice in Wonderland*, cited by Harlan Cleveland in "A Passion for Paradox," in the Maxwell Summer Lecture Series, "Reflections on Public Policy" (Syracuse, N.Y., Syracuse University, Maxwell Graduate School, 1977).

INDEX

This index has been constructed to emphasize ideas presented in the text. Entries reflect the project process, that is, identification, design, and implementation of projects. Cross-referencing between "project" and "cultural" entries has been employed. Entries have been made on the basis of their importance to the shared concerns of project managers and social scientists. Neither the names of countries nor the names of persons have been included unless the relevant text material is at least one or more sentences in length.

ABOUT THE AUTHOR

Glynn Cochrane is Professor of Anthropology and Public Administration, and Chairman of the Department of Anthropology, in the Maxwell Graduate School at Syracuse University. He is an expert on the use of anthropology in international development assistance, and serves as a consultant to the United Nations, the World Bank, and the U.S. AID.

Before joining the Syracuse University faculty, Professor Cochrane served for six years as an administrative officer in the British Overseas Civil Service, he was stationed in England and in the South Pacific. He later studied social anthropology at Oxford University and received his doctorate in 1967.

Professor Cochrane is the author of *Big Men and Cargo Cults, Development Anthropology,* and *What We Can Do for Each Other.* He has written numerous papers on development topics, which have appeared in such professional journals as *Journal of Developing Areas, Human Organization,* and *American Anthropologist.*

The present book is an extended treatment of the project appraisal system, called Social Soundness Analysis, which Professor Cochrane wrote for AID in 1974, and which is now used extensively by the U.S. agency in overseas project work.

RELATED TITLES
Published by
Praeger Special Studies

Organization for Rural Development: Risk Taking and
Appropriate Technology
> *Allen D. Jedlicka*

Rural Communities: Inter-Cooperation and Development
> *edited by*
> *Yehuda H. Landau*
> *Maurice Konopnicki*
> *Henri Desroche*
> *Placide Rambaud*

A Behavioral Study of Rural Modernization: Social and
Economic Change in Thai Villages
> *Charles A. Murray*

Urbanization and Rural Development: A Spatial Policy
for Equitable Growth
> *Dennis A. Rondinelli*
> *Kenneth Ruddle*

Decision Making in Developing Countries: Multiobjective
Formulation and Evaluation Methods
> *Alfredo Sfeir-Younis*
> *Daniel W. Bromley*

**Small-Scale Employment and Production in Developing
Countries:** Evidence from Ghana
> *William F. Steel*